SUPER COOKERY

Wok & Oriental

p

This is a Parragon Publishing Book
This edition published in 2002

Parragon Publishing
Queen Street House
4 Queen Street
Bath BA1 1HE, UK

ISBN: 0-75257-563-5

A copy of the CIP data for this book is available from the British
Library, upon request.

Printed in China

Note
Cup measurements used in this book are for American cups.
Tablespoons are assumed to be 15 ml. Unless otherwise stated,
milk is assumed to be full fat, eggs are medium, and pepper is
freshly ground black pepper.

Contents

Introduction

Asian cookery basically requires the use of a wok. If you have one, then a whole array of wonderful dishes are open to you. It is worth buying a wok, rather than using a skillet, for more satisfactory results when trying the delicious range of recipes which follow in this book.

Basically, a wok is a curved, shallow, bowl-like cooking implement which is made of metal and has either a single long, wooden handle or two looped handles at opposite sides of the pan. It comes in many sizes, but the most appropriate for a family is approximately 12-14 inches in diameter. It may be made from stainless steel, cast iron or copper, the cast iron, being the better choice as it retains heat more efficiently, especially when well-seasoned. There are numerous advantages to a wok over a skillet. The convex shape means that food is easily moved around the wok and tossed (the basis of stir-frying), and cooks much more quickly. It can easily be tilted if required or rotated to reach ingredients easily.

Owing to the curved sides of the wok, the heat rises and the whole wok becomes a hot cooking surface. It therefore conserves fuel and is perfect for quick cooking and stir-frying. Cleaning is no problem as there are no corners or edges in which food can become lodged.

USEFUL EQUIPMENT

There are several other pieces of equipment that will be useful with a wok. One of the most important in the Western kitchen is a *collar*. Basically this is a metal crown with angled sides and hollows which aids heat convection from our modern hobs and cooking rings. The wok sits in the collar and gives more even cooking than if it were simply placed on an electric ring. A *long-handled spatula* is useful for cooking and removing foods as the curved edge follows the curve of the wok. Be sure to buy one with a wooden handle to insulate your hands from the heat.

The wok is mainly used for stir-frying, but may also be used for deep-frying and steaming. A *frying strainer* or *shallow wire-meshed basket* is useful to remove foods from fat and a *steaming trivet* will convert your wok to a steamer.

Obviously a *lid* is essential for some wok cooking, and should be domed and fitted snugly inside the wok to seal in the flavors during steaming. Many boxed wok sets contain all of these additional pieces of equipment as they are an essential part of wok cooking if it is to be used to its full potential.

USING YOUR WOK

Before using your wok, it is essential to season it as with other pans. Wipe the wok inside and out with oiled paper towels and heat it to a high heat in the oven or on the hob. Remove the wok from the heat, allow it to cool and repeat this process several times to give a good coating—this will make it

4

easier to clean and give it a nonstick coating. After the initial seasoning, the wok may be cleaned with soap and water, but it must be dried immediately if made of cast iron, to prevent it from rusting. Generally, the wok is simply wiped clean, and allowed to blacken with use. It is said that the blacker the wok, the better the cook, as it shows how frequently the wok is used.

STIR-FRYING

The wok is most widely used for stir-frying, a cooking method which originated in China, and remains the most recognized form of Chinese cooking. This method has spread throughout East Asia. In China it is called *Ch'au*, which primarily means one or a number of ingredients are sliced thinly and evenly and cooked in 1–2 tablespoons of fat.

The food is stirred with long bamboo chopsticks or a spatula and seasonings and sauces may be added.

Stir-frying is often done in stages. This allows foods which have longer cooking times to be stir-fried and removed, and then returned to the wok at a later stage, and also for individual flavors to be kept distinct. The dish is always brought together at the end of cooking in the wok and served as a whole. Usually peanut or corn oil are used to fry the foods, but occasionally chicken fat and sometimes lard will be used for more delicate flavors.

There are different types of stir-frying which are described below:

Liu is wet frying with less vigorous stirring and more turning of the foods. A cornstarch and stock mixture is added with sugar, vinegar, and soy sauce at the end of cooking for a delicious coating sauce.

Pao, or 'explosion', requires foods to be fried at the highest heat, and it is a very short, sharp method of cooking, usually lasting only 1 minute. Foods cooked in this way are generally marinated beforehand for flavor and tenderness.

WOK COOKING AROUND THE WORLD

Across the Far East woks are used in various guises for many dishes. In India, a large pan or *karahi* is used which sits over a hole in a brick or earth oven. This wok-like vessel is used for braising and frying, the infamous curry or *karahi* deriving its name from the pan. In Indonesia, a *wajan* or wok is used over wood or charcoal for curries, rice dishes, and quick stir-fries—the same applies in Japan, Thailand, Singapore, and Malaysia, all of which have been influenced by Chinese cooking. Even a Mongolian barbecue resembles a wok, being a convex iron griddle.

You will gather from the preceding information that the wok and the stir-frying cooking methods are both essential and unique to Asian and Far Eastern cooking, being swift, light, healthy, and extremely versatile. The following recipes take you on a magical journey of the Far East, covering soups, starters, meat and poultry, fabulous fish dishes, vegetarian dishes, and, of course, rice and noodles, the staples in these countries. So get out your wok and prepare yourself for the feast of flavors now open to you!

In the West we tend to talk about Chinese cooking as a generalization, as though it were the same throughout China. In fact, China is a vast country, with a range of topography and climates that produce distinct regional differences.

This book contains recipes that are popular in both China and the West. Dishes from Szechwan in the west, Canton in the south, Beijing in the north, and Shanghai in the east offer an array of different flavors and cooking methods. The dishes included in this book range from hot and spicy to delicate flavors using fish and vegetables, with a mid-range of sweet-and-sour dishes, rice, noodles, and a small section of desserts.

One of the most important features of Chinese cooking is texture. Vegetables should remain crisp, and rice and noodles should be treated like pasta, and retain their 'bite' after cooking. Ingredients such as bean curd are used for texture, even though they have little flavor. Bamboo shoots, a common ingredient, are included purely for texture.

Although the Chinese make use of fresh foods, they also use dried foodstuffs in their recipes, in particular mushrooms, bean curd, noodles, and spices.

COOKING METHODS

The Chinese combine a couple of cooking methods in one dish, such as steaming and then frying, or frying and roasting, but little special equipment is required.

Steaming is widely used in Chinese cookery. Traditionally bamboo steamers are used, so that a whole meal may be cooked in one stack of bamboo racks. The rice is usually placed in the bottom and different dishes stacked on top, those taking the longest to cook being placed at the bottom. If you do not have a steamer, invert a heatproof plate in a large saucepan, and cover it with a lid. Boiling water is added to the steamer, to cover one third of the depth of the dish. This water may need topping up during cooking, although many of the dishes cook very quickly. Steaming is a very healthy method of cooking, not using any fat, and it traps the flavors of the dish.

Stir-frying is done in a wok that must be heated before use. Foods of similar size (all small) are stirred constantly, so that as they come into contact with the wok, they cook quickly. Sometimes foods are cooked in batches and removed. This is to preserve flavors. The dishes are always brought together in the wok at the end of cooking, and may have sauces added during or at the end of the cooking time, depending on the region from which they originated. Peanut oil is usually used for stir-frying, but vegetable oil may be used in its place.

Deep-frying is also done in the wok, which uses less oil than a deep-fryer. The shape of the wok allows oil to drain from the food into the center of the wok. The foods are often marinated first or coated in a light batter. Quick-frying is also used, whereby foods are either fried on one side (used for noodles), and not turned, or turned once and sliced for serving.

USEFUL CHINESE INGREDIENTS

Bamboo shoots *These are added for texture, as they have very little flavor. Available in cans, they are a common ingredient in Chinese cooking.*

Bean curd *This soya bean paste is available in several forms. The cake variety, which is soft, and spongy, and a white-gray color, is used in this book. It is very bland, but adds texture to dishes and is perfect for absorbing all the other flavors in the dish.*

Beansprouts *These are mung bean shoots, which are very nutritious, containing many vitamins. They add crunch to a recipe and are widely available. Do not overcook them, as they wilt, and do not add texture to the dish.*

Black beans *These are soy beans and are very salty. They can be bought and crushed with salt, and then rinsed, or used in the form of a ready-made sauce for convenience.*

Chinese beans *These long beans may be eaten whole and are very tender. Green beans may also be used.*

Chinese five-spice powder *An aromatic blend of cinnamon, cloves, star anise, fennel, and brown peppercorns. It is often used in marinades.*

Chinese leaves *A light green leaf with a sweet flavor. It can be found readily in most supermarkets.*

Hoisin sauce *A dark brown, sweet, thick sauce that is widely available. It is made from spices, soy sauce, garlic, and chili and is often served as a dipping sauce.*

Litchis *These are worth buying fresh, as they are easy to prepare. Inside the inedible skin is a fragrant white flesh. Litchis are available tinned and are a classic ingredient.*

Mango *Choose a ripe mango for its sweet, scented flesh. If a mango is underripe when bought, leave it in a sunny place for a few days before using.*

Noodles *The Chinese use several varieties of noodle. You will probably find it easier to use the readily available dried varieties, such as egg noodles, which are yellow, rice stick noodles, which are white and very fine, or transparent noodles, which are opaque when dry and turn transparent on cooking. However, cellophane or rice noodles may be used instead.*

Oyster sauce *Readily available, this sauce is made from oysters, salt, seasonings, and cornstarch, and is brown in color.*

Pak choi *Also known as Chinese cabbage, this has a mild, slightly bitter, flavor.*

Rice vinegar *This has a mild, sweet taste that is quite delicate. It is available in some supermarkets, but if not available, use cider vinegar instead.*

Rice wine *This is similar to dry sherry in color, alcohol content, and smell, but it is worth buying rice wine for its distinctive flavor.*

Sesame oil *This is made from roasted sesame seeds and has an intense flavor. It burns easily and is therefore added at the end of cooking for flavor, and is not used for frying.*

Soy sauce *This is widely available, but it is worth buying a good grade of sauce. It is produced in both light and dark varieties—the former is used with fish and vegetables for a lighter color and flavor, while the latter, being darker, richer, saltier, and more intense, is used as a dipping sauce or with strongly flavored meats.*

Star anise *This is an eight-pointed, star-shaped pod with a strong aniseed flavor. The spice is also available ground. If a pod is added to a dish, it should be removed before serving.*

Szechwan pepper *This is quite hot and spicy, and should be used sparingly. It is red in color and is readily available.*

Water chestnuts *These are flat and round and can usually only be purchased in cans, already peeled. They add a delicious crunch to dishes and have a sweet flavor.*

Yellow beans *Again a soy bean and very salty. Use a variety that is chunky rather than smooth.*

Soups & Starters

Soup is indispensable at Asian tables, especially in China, Japan, Korea, and South East Asia. Chicken soup, for example, is sometimes served in China, Malaysia, and Thailand for breakfast! However, it is generally eaten part way through a main meal to clear the palate for further dishes, but it is never served as a starter as in the Western world. There are many different types of delicious soups, both thick and thin and, of course, the clear soups which are often served with wontons or dumplings in them. In Japan, the clear soups are exquisite arrangements of fish, meat, and vegetables in a clear broth.

Starters or snacks are drier foods in general, such as spring rolls, which come in many variations and shapes across the Far East. Satay is served in Indonesia, Malaysia, and Thailand, and other delights are wrapped in pastry, bread, rice paper, or skewered for ease of eating. Again these are generally served as snacks in their native countries, but are frequent starters in Western restaurants.

The following chapter contains many delicious recipes for both soups and starters, all of which are the perfect way to begin a meal and whet the appetite for the delicious dishes that follow.

Spicy Chicken Noodle Soup

Serves 4

INGREDIENTS

2 tbsp tamarind paste

4 red Thai chiles, finely chopped

2 cloves garlic, crushed

1-inch piece Thai ginger, peeled and very finely chopped

4 tbsp fish sauce

2 tbsp palm sugar or brown sugar

8 lime leaves, roughly torn

5 cups chicken stock

12 ounces boneless chicken breast

1–2 medium carrots, very thinly sliced

12 ounces sweet potato, diced

3½ ounces baby corn cobs, halved

3 tbsp fresh cilantro, roughly chopped

3½ ounces cherry tomatoes, halved

5½ ounces flat rice noodles

fresh cilantro, chopped, to garnish

1 Place the tamarind paste, Thai chiles, garlic, Thai ginger, fish sauce, sugar, lime leaves, and chicken stock in a large preheated wok and bring to a boil, stirring constantly. Reduce the heat and cook for about 5 minutes.

2 Using a sharp knife, thinly slice the chicken. Add the chicken to the wok and cook for a further 5 minutes, stirring the mixture well.

3 Reduce the heat slightly and add the carrots, sweet potato, and baby corn cobs to the wok. Simmer, uncovered, for about 5 minutes, or until the vegetables are just tender and the chicken is completely cooked through.

4 Stir in the cilantro, cherry tomatoes and noodles. Simmer for about 5 minutes, or until the noodles are tender. Transfer to warm bowls, garnish and serve hot.

COOK'S TIP

Tamarind paste is produced from the seed pod of the tamarind tree. It adds both a brown color and tang to soups and gravies. If unavailable, dilute brown sugar or molasses with lime juice.

Crab & Corn Noodle Soup

Serves 4

INGREDIENTS

1 tbsp sunflower oil
1 tsp Chinese five-spice powder
3-4 medium carrots, cut into
　　sticks
$^1/_2$ cup canned or frozen corn

$^3/_4$ cup peas
6 scallions, trimmed and sliced
1 red chili, seeded and very
　　thinly sliced

2 x 7 ounce can white crab meat
6 ounces egg noodles
$7^1/_2$ cups fish stock
3 tbsp soy sauce

1 Heat the sunflower oil in a large preheated wok.

2 Add the Chinese five-spice powder, carrots, sweetcorn, peas, scallions and chili to the wok and stir fry for about 5 minutes.

3 Add the crab meat to the wok and stir-fry the mixture for 1 minute.

4 Roughly break up the egg noodles and add to the wok.

5 Pour the stock and soy sauce into the mixture in the wok, bring to the boil, cover and leave to simmer for 5 minutes.

6 Transfer the soup to warm serving bowls and serve at once.

COOK'S TIP

Chinese five-spice powder is a mixture of star anise, fennel, cloves, cinnamon, and Szechuan pepper.

COOK'S TIP

Use thin egg noodles for the best result in this recipe.

Spicy Thai Soup with Shrimp

Serves 4

INGREDIENTS
---

2 tbsp tamarind paste

4 red Thai chiles, very finely chopped

2 cloves garlic, crushed

1 inch piece Thai ginger, peeled and very finely chopped

4 tbsp fish sauce

2 tbsp palm sugar or brown sugar

8 lime leaves, roughly torn

5 cups fish stock

1–2 medium carrots, very thinly sliced

12 ounces sweet potato, diced

1 cup baby corn cobs, halved

3 tbsp fresh cilantro, roughly chopped

3 1/2 ounces cherry tomatoes, halved

8 ounces fan-tail shrimp

---

1 Place the tamarind paste, Thai chiles, garlic, ginger, fish sauce, palm or brown sugar, lime leaves, and fish stock in a large preheated wok. Bring to a boil, stirring constantly.

2 Reduce the heat and add the carrot, sweet potato, and baby corn to the mixture in the wok.

3 Simmer the soup, uncovered, for about 10 minutes, or until the vegetables are just tender.

4 Stir the cilantro, cherry tomatoes, and shrimp into the soup and heat through for about 5 minutes.

5 Transfer the soup to warm serving bowls and serve hot.

COOK'S TIP

Palm sugar is a thick, coarse brown sugar that has a slightly caramel taste. It is sold in round cakes.

COOK'S TIP

Thai ginger or galangal is a member of the ginger family, but it is yellow in color with pink sprouts. The flavor is aromatic and less pungent than ginger.

Coconut & Crab Soup

Serves 4

INGREDIENTS

1 tbsp peanut oil

2 tbsp Thai red curry paste

1 red bell pepper, seeded and sliced

2¹/₂ cups coconut milk

2¹/₂ cups fish stock

2 tbsp fish sauce

8 ounces canned or fresh white
crab meat

8 ounces fresh or frozen crab claws

2 tbsp chopped fresh cilantro

3 scallions, trimmed and sliced

1 Heat the oil in a large preheated wok.

2 Add the red curry paste and red bell pepper to the wok and stir-fry for 1 minute.

3 Add the coconut milk, fish stock, and fish sauce to the wok and bring to a boil.

4 Add the crab meat (drained if canned), crab claws (thawed if frozen), cilantro, and scallions to the wok. Stir the mixture well and heat thoroughly for 2–3 minutes.

5 Transfer the soup to warm bowls and serve hot.

COOK'S TIP

Coconut milk adds a sweet and creamy flavor to the dish. It is available in powdered form or in cans ready to use.

COOK'S TIP

Clean the wok after each use by washing it with water, using a mild detergent if necessary, and a soft cloth or brush. Do not scrub or use any abrasive cleaner, as this will scratch the surface. Dry thoroughly with paper towels or over a low heat, then wipe the surface all over with a little oil. This forms a sealing layer to protect the surface of the wok from moisture and prevents it rusting.

Chili Fish Soup

Serves 4

INGREDIENTS

½ ounce Chinese dried
    mushrooms
2 tbsp sunflower oil
1 onion, sliced

1½ cups snow peas
1½ cups bamboo shoots
3 tbsp sweet chili sauce
5 cups fish or vegetable stock

3 tbsp light soy sauce
2 tbsp fresh cilantro
1 pound cod fillet, skinned and
    cubed

1 Place the mushrooms in a large bowl. Pour over enough boiling water to cover and let stand for 5 minutes. Drain the mushrooms thoroughly. Using a sharp knife, remove the stalks and roughly chop the caps.

2 Heat the sunflower oil in a preheated wok. Add the onion to the wok and stir-fry for 5 minutes, or until softened.

3 Add the snow peas, bamboo shoots, chili sauce, stock, and soy sauce to the wok and bring to a boil.

4 Add the cilantro and cubed fish to the wok. Lower the heat slightly and simmer for about 5 minutes, or until the fish is cooked through.

5 Transfer the soup to warm bowls, garnish with extra cilantro, if wished, and serve hot.

VARIATION

Cod is used in this recipe, as it is a meaty white fish. For real luxury, use monkfish tail instead.

COOK'S TIP

There are many different varieties of dried mushrooms, but shiitake are best. They are not cheap, but a small quantity will go a long way.

Hot & Sour Mushroom Soup

Serves 4

INGREDIENTS

2 tbsp tamarind paste

4 red Thai chiles, very finely chopped

2 cloves garlic, crushed

1-inch piece of Thai ginger, peeled and very finely chopped

4 tbsp fish sauce

2 tbsp palm or brown sugar

8 lime leaves, roughly torn

5 cups vegetable stock

1–2 medium carrots, very thinly sliced

3¼ cups button mushrooms, halved

12 ounces shredded white cabbage

¾ cup fine green beans, halved

3 tbsp fresh cilantro, roughly chopped

3½ ounces cherry tomatoes, halved

1 Place the tamarind paste, Thai chiles, garlic, Thai ginger, fish sauce, palm or brown sugar, lime leaves, and stock in a large preheated wok. Bring the mixture to a boil, stirring occasionally.

2 Reduce the heat slightly and add the carrots, mushrooms, cabbage, and green beans. Simmer the soup, uncovered, for about 10 minutes, or until the vegetables are just tender.

3 Stir the cilantro and cherry tomatoes into the mixture in the wok and heat through for 5 minutes.

4 Transfer the soup to warm bowls and serve hot.

COOK'S TIP

Tamarind is one of the ingredients that gives Thai cuisine its special sweet and sour flavor.

VARIATION

Instead of the white cabbage, try using Chinese cabbage for a sweeter flavor. Add the Chinese cabbage with the cilantro and cherry tomatoes in step 3.

Chicken Wonton Soup

Serves 4–6

INGREDIENTS

FILLING:

12 ounces ground chicken

1 tablespoon soy sauce

1 teaspoon grated, fresh ginger root

1 garlic clove, crushed

2 teaspoons sherry

2 scallions, chopped

1 teaspoon sesame oil

1 egg white

½ teaspoon cornstarch

½ teaspoon sugar

about 35 wonton wrappers

SOUP:

6 cups chicken stock

1 tablespoon light soy sauce

1 scallion, shredded

1 small carrot, cut into very thin
    slices

1 Combine all the ingredients for the filling and mix well.

2 Place a small spoonful of the filling in the center of each wonton wrapper.

3 Dampen the edges and gather up the wonton wrapper to form a pouch enclosing the filling.

4 Cook the filled wontons in boiling water for 1 minute, or until they float to the top.

5 Remove with a slotted spoon. Bring the chicken stock to a boil.

6 Add the soy sauce, shredded scallion, carrot, and wontons to the soup. Simmer gently for 2 minutes, then serve.

VARIATION

Instead of the chicken, you can use ground pork.

COOK'S TIP

Look for wonton wrappers in Chinese or Asian supermarkets. Fresh wrappers can be found in the chilled compartment and they can be frozen if desired. Wrap them in plastic wrap before freezing.

Clear Chicken & Egg Soup

Serves 4

INGREDIENTS

1 tsp salt	1 leek, sliced	2 open-cap mushrooms, sliced
1 tbsp rice wine vinegar	4¹⁄₂ ounces broccoli florets	1 tbsp dry sherry
4 eggs	1 cup shredded	dash of chili sauce
3³⁄₄ cups chicken stock	cooked chicken	chili powder, to garnish

1 Bring a large saucepan of water to a boil and add the salt and rice wine vinegar. Reduce the heat so that it is just simmering and carefully break the eggs into the water, one at a time. Poach the eggs for 1 minute. Remove the poached eggs with a slotted spoon and set aside.

2 Bring the chicken stock to a boil in a separate pan and add the leek, broccoli, chicken, mushrooms, and sherry, and season with chili sauce to taste. Cook for 10–15 minutes.

3 Add the poached eggs to the soup and cook for a further 2 minutes. Carefully transfer the soup and poached eggs to 4 individual soup bowls. Dust with a little chili powder to garnish and serve immediately.

COOK'S TIP

You could substitute 4¹⁄₂ ounces fresh or canned crab meat or the same quantity of fresh or frozen cooked shrimp for the chicken, if desired.

VARIATION

You could use 4 dried Chinese mushrooms, rehydrated according to the package instructions, instead of the open-cap mushrooms, if desired.

Curried Chicken & Corn Soup

Serves 4

INGREDIENTS

6 ounce can corn, drained
$3^3/_4$ cups chicken stock
12 ounces cooked, lean chicken,
   cut into strips

16 baby corncobs
1 tsp Chinese curry powder
$^1/_2$-inch piece fresh ginger
   root, grated

3 tbsp light soy sauce
2 tbsp chopped chives

1 Place the canned corn in a food processor, together with $^2/_3$ cup of the chicken stock and process until the mixture forms a smooth purée.

2 Rub the corn purée through a fine strainer, pressing with the back of a spoon to remove any husks.

3 Pour the remaining chicken stock into a large saucepan and add the strips of cooked chicken. Stir in the corn purée.

4 Add the baby corncobs and bring the soup to a boil. Boil the soup for 10 minutes.

5 Add the curry powder, grated ginger, and soy sauce and cook for a further 10–15 minutes. Stir in the chopped chives.

6 Transfer the soup to warm individual soup bowls and serve immediately.

COOK'S TIP

Prepare the soup up to 24 hours in advance without adding the chicken, cool, cover, and store in the refrigerator. Add the chicken and heat the soup through thoroughly before serving.

Hot & Sour Soup

Serves 4

INGREDIENTS

2 tbsp cornstarch	1 small fresh red chili,	3³/₄ cups chicken or beef
4 tbsp water	finely chopped	consommé
2 tbsp light soy sauce	1 egg	1 open-cap mushroom, sliced
3 tbsp rice wine vinegar	2 tbsp vegetable oil	1³/₄ ounces skinless chicken breast,
¹/₂ tsp ground black pepper	1 onion, chopped	cut into very thin strips
		1 tsp sesame oil

1 Blend the cornstarch with the water to form a smooth paste. Add the soy sauce, rice wine vinegar, pepper, and chili and mix together well.

2 Break the egg into a separate bowl and beat well.

3 Heat the oil in a preheated wok and stir-fry the onion for 1–2 minutes.

4 Stir in the consommé, mushroom, and chicken and bring to a boil. Cook for about 15 minutes, or until the chicken is tender.

5 Pour the cornstarch mixture into the soup and cook the soup, stirring constantly, until it has thickened.

6 As you are stirring, gradually drizzle the egg into the soup, to create threads of egg.

7 Sprinkle with the sesame oil and serve immediately.

COOK'S TIP

Make sure that the egg is poured in very slowly and that you stir continuously to create threads of egg and not large pieces.

Peking Duck Soup

Serves 4

INGREDIENTS

4 1/2 ounces lean duck breast
8 ounces Chinese cabbage
3 3/4 cups chicken or duck stock
1 tbsp dry sherry or rice wine

1 tbsp light soy sauce
2 garlic cloves, crushed
pinch of ground star anise

1 tbsp sesame seeds
1 tsp sesame oil
1 tbsp chopped fresh parsley

1 Remove the skin from the duck breast and finely dice the flesh.

2 Using a sharp knife, shred the Chinese cabbage.

3 Put the stock in a large saucepan and bring to a boil.

4 Add the sherry or rice wine, soy sauce, diced duck meat, and shredded Chinese cabbage and stir to mix thoroughly. Reduce the heat and simmer gently for 15 minutes.

5 Stir in the garlic and star anise and cook over a low heat for a further 10–15 minutes, or until the duck is tender.

6 Meanwhile, dry-fry the sesame seeds in a preheated, heavy-based skillet or wok, stirring constantly.

7 Remove the sesame seeds from the pan and stir them into the soup, together with the sesame oil and parsley.

8 Spoon the soup into warm bowls and serve immediately.

COOK'S TIP

If Chinese cabbage is unavailable, use leafy green cabbage instead. You may wish to adjust the quantity to taste, as Western cabbage has a stronger flavor and odor than Chinese cabbage.

Beef & Vegetable Noodle Soup

Serves 4

INGREDIENTS

8 ounces lean beef	1 tsp sesame oil	$\frac{1}{2}$ leek, shredded
1 garlic clove, crushed	8 ounces egg noodles	$4\frac{1}{2}$ ounces broccoli, cut
2 scallions, chopped	$3\frac{3}{4}$ cups beef stock	into florets
3 tbsp soy sauce	3 baby corncobs, sliced	pinch of chili powder

1 Using a sharp knife, cut the beef into very thin strips and place them in a shallow glass bowl or dish.

2 Add the garlic, scallions, soy sauce, and sesame oil and mix together well, turning the beef to coat. Cover and marinate in the refrigerator for 30 minutes.

3 Cook the noodles in a saucepan of boiling water for 3–4 minutes. Drain the noodles thoroughly and set aside until they are required.

4 Put the beef stock in a large saucepan and bring to a boil.

5 Add the beef, together with the marinade, the baby corn, leek, and broccoli. Cover and simmer over a low heat for 7–10 minutes, or until the beef and vegetables are tender and cooked through.

6 Stir in the noodles and chili powder and cook for a further 2–3 minutes. Transfer to bowls and serve immediately.

COOK'S TIP

Vary the vegetables used, or use those on hand. If desired, use a few drops of chili sauce instead of chili powder, but remember it is very hot!

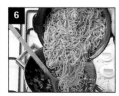

Lamb & Rice Soup

Serves 4

> **INGREDIENTS**

5½ ounces lean lamb
¼ cup rice
3¾ cups lamb stock
1 leek, sliced

1 garlic clove, thinly sliced
2 tsp light soy sauce
1 tsp rice wine vinegar

1 medium open-cap mushroom,
thinly sliced
salt

1 Using a sharp knife, trim any fat from the lamb and cut the meat into thin strips. Set aside until required.

2 Bring a large pan of lightly salted water to a boil and add the rice. Bring back to a boil, stir once, reduce the heat, and cook for 10–15 minutes, until tender. Drain, rinse under cold running water, drain again, and set aside until required.

3 Meanwhile, put the lamb stock in a large saucepan and bring to a boil.

4 Add the lamb strips, leek, garlic, soy sauce, and rice wine vinegar to the stock in the pan. Reduce the heat, cover, and simmer for 10 minutes, or until the lamb is tender and thoroughly cooked through.

5 Add the mushroom slices and the rice to the pan and cook for a further 2–3 minutes, or until the mushroom is completely cooked through.

6 Ladle the soup into 4 individual warm soup bowls and serve immediately.

COOK'S TIP

Use a few dried Chinese mushrooms, rehydrated according to the package instructions and chopped, as an alternative to the open-cap mushroom. Add the Chinese mushrooms with the lamb in step 4.

Fish Soup with Wontons

Serves 4

INGREDIENTS

4½ ounces large, cooked, peeled shrimp
1 tsp chopped chives
1 small garlic clove, finely chopped

1 tbsp vegetable oil
12 wonton wrappers
1 small egg, beaten
3¾ cups fish stock

6 ounces white fish fillet, diced
dash of chili sauce
sliced fresh red chili and chives, to garnish

1 Roughly chop about one quarter of the shrimp and mix together with the chopped chives and garlic.

2 Heat the oil in a preheated wok and stir-fry the shrimp mixture for 1–2 minutes. Remove from the heat and set aside to cool completely.

3 Spread out the wonton wrappers on a counter. Spoon a little of the shrimp filling into the center of each wrapper. Brush the edges of the wrappers with beaten egg and press the edges together, scrunching them to form a "moneybag" shape. Set the wontons aside while you are preparing the soup.

4 Pour the fish stock into a large saucepan and bring to a boil. Add the diced white fish and the remaining shrimp and cook for 5 minutes.

5 Season to taste with the chili sauce. Add the wontons and cook for a further 5 minutes. Spoon into warm serving bowls, garnish with sliced red chili and chives, and serve immediately.

VARIATION

Replace the shrimp with cooked crab meat for an alternative flavor.

Crab & Ginger Soup

Serves 4

INGREDIENTS

1 carrot, peeled and chopped	2 medium-size cooked crabs	1 tsp light soy sauce
1 leek, chopped	1-inch piece fresh ginger root,	$\frac{1}{2}$ tsp ground star anise
1 bay leaf	grated	salt and pepper
$3\frac{3}{4}$ cups fish stock		

1 Put the carrot, leek, bay leaf, and fish stock into a saucepan and bring to a boil. Reduce the heat, cover, and simmer for about 10 minutes.

2 Meanwhile, remove the meat from the crabs. Break off the claws and legs, break the joints, and remove the meat. Discard the gills, split the bodies open, and scoop out all the meat. Add the crab meat to the saucepan of fish stock.

3 Add the ginger, soy sauce, and star anise to the fish stock and bring to a boil. Simmer for about 10 minutes, or until the vegetables are tender and the crab is heated through. Season to taste with salt and pepper. Ladle the soup into warm individual bowls and serve immediately.

4 Ladle the soup into warmed serving bowls and garnish with crab claws. Serve at once.

COOK'S TIP

If fresh crab meat is unavailable, use drained canned crab meat or thawed frozen crab meat instead.

COOK'S TIP

To prepare cooked crab, loosen the meat from the shell by banging the back of the underside with a clenched fist. Stand the crab on its edge with the shell toward you. Force the shell from the body with your thumbs. Twist off the legs and claws and remove the meat. Twist off the tail and discard. Remove and discard the gills from each side of the body. Cut the body in half along the center and remove all of the meat. Scoop the brown meat from the shell with a spoon.

Shrimp Dumpling Soup

Serves 4

INGREDIENTS

DUMPLINGS:

1 ⅝ cups all-purpose flour
¼ cup boiling water
1/8 cup cold water
1½ tsp vegetable oil

FILLING:

4½ ounces ground pork
4½ ounces cooked, peeled
    shrimp, chopped
1¾ ounces canned water chestnuts,
    drained, rinsed, and chopped
1 celery stalk, chopped
1 tsp cornstarch
1 tbsp sesame oil
1 tbsp light soy sauce

SOUP:

3¾ cups fish stock
1¾ ounces cellophane noodles
1 tbsp dry sherry
chopped chives, to garnish

1 To make the dumplings, mix together the flour, boiling water, cold water, and oil in a bowl until a pliable dough is formed.

2 Knead the dough on a lightly floured surface for 5 minutes. Cut the dough into 16 equal-size pieces.

3 Roll the dough pieces into rounds about 3 inches in diameter.

4 Mix the filling ingredients together in a large bowl.

5 Spoon a little of the filling mixture into the center of each round. Bring the edges of the dough together, scrunching them up to form a "moneybag" shape. Twist to seal.

6 Pour the fish stock into a large saucepan and bring to a boil.

7 Add the cellophane noodles, dumplings, and dry sherry to the pan and cook for 4–5 minutes, until the noodles and dumplings are tender. Garnish with chopped chives and serve immediately.

COOK'S TIP

Wonton wrappers may be used instead of the dumpling dough if time is short.

Chinese Cabbage Soup

Serves 4

INGREDIENTS

1 pound bok choy	1 tbsp light soy sauce	1 fresh red chili, thinly sliced
2½ cups vegetable stock	1 tbsp superfine sugar	1 tbsp cornstarch
1 tbsp rice wine vinegar	1 tbsp dry sherry	2 tbsp water

1 Using a sharp knife, trim the stems of the bok choy and shred the leaves.

2 Heat the stock in a large saucepan. Add the bok choy and cook for 10–15 minutes.

3 Mix the rice wine vinegar, soy sauce, sugar, and sherry together. Add this mixture to the stock, together with the sliced chili. Bring to a boil, lower the heat, and cook for 2–3 minutes.

4 Blend the cornstarch with the water to form a smooth paste. Gradually stir the cornstarch mixture into the soup. Cook, stirring constantly, until it has thickened. Cook for a further 4–5 minutes. Ladle the soup into individual warm serving bowls and serve immediately.

VARIATION

Boil about 2 tbsp rice in lightly salted water until tender. Drain and spoon into the base of the soup bowls. Ladle the soup over the rice and serve immediately.

COOK'S TIP

Bok choy, also known as pak choi or spoon cabbage, has long, white leaf stalks and fleshy, spoon-shaped, shiny green leaves. There are a number of varieties available, which differ mainly in size rather than flavor.

Thai-Style Spicy Corn Fritters

Serves 4

INGREDIENTS

1⅓ cup canned or frozen corn

2 red Thai chiles, seeded and very finely chopped

2 cloves garlic, crushed

10 lime leaves, very finely chopped

2 tbsp fresh cilantro, chopped

1 large egg

½ cup cornmeal

¾ cup fine green beans, very finely sliced

peanut oil, for frying

1 Place the corn, chiles, garlic, lime leaves, cilantro, egg, and cornmeal in a large mixing bowl, and stir to combine.

2 Add the green beans to the ingredients in the bowl and mix well, using a wooden spoon.

3 Divide the cornmeal mixture into small, even-size balls. Flatten the balls of mixture between the palms of your hands to form rounds.

4 Heat a little peanut oil in a preheated wok.

5 Fry the fritters, in batches, until brown and crispy on the outside, turning occasionally.

6 Transfer the corn fritters to warm serving plates and serve immediately.

COOK'S TIP

If using canned corn, drain thoroughly and then rinse, and drain thoroughly again before use.

COOK'S TIP

Kaffir lime leaves are dark green, glossy leaves that have a lemony-lime flavor. They can be bought from specialty Asian stores either fresh or dried. Fresh leaves impart the most delicious flavor.

Vegetable Spring Rolls

Serves 4

INGREDIENTS

3-4 medium carrots
1 red bell pepper
1 tbsp sunflower oil, plus extra
    for frying
$\frac{1}{2}$ cup bean sprouts
finely grated zest and juice of 1 lime

1 red chili, seeded and very
    finely chopped
1 tbsp soy sauce
$\frac{1}{2}$ tsp arrowroot
2 tbsp chopped fresh cilantro

8 sheets filo pastry
2 tbsp butter
2 tsp sesame oil
scallion tassels, to garnish
chili sauce, to serve

1 Using a sharp knife, cut the carrots into thin sticks. Seed the bell pepper and cut the flesh into thin slices.

2 Heat the sunflower oil in a large preheated wok.

3 Add the carrot, red bell pepper, and bean sprouts and cook, stirring, for 2 minutes, or until softened. Remove the wok from the heat and toss in the lime zest and juice, and the red chili.

4 Mix the soy sauce with the arrowroot. Stir the mixture into the wok, return to the heat, and cook for 2 minutes, or until the juices thicken. Add the cilantro and mix well.

5 Lay the sheets of filo pastry out on a board. Melt the butter with the sesame oil and brush each sheet with the mixture. Spoon a little of the vegetable filling at the top of each sheet, fold over each long side, and roll up.

6 Add a little oil to the wok and cook the spring rolls, in batches, for 2–3 minutes, or until crisp and golden. Garnish with scallion tassels and serve hot with chili dipping sauce.

COOK'S TIP

Use prepared spring roll skins available from Chinese supermarkets or healthfood shops instead of the filo pastry if desired.

Seven-Spice Eggplants

Serves 4

INGREDIENTS

1 pound eggplants, wiped	7 tbsp cornstarch	1 tbsp Thai seven-spice seasoning
1 egg white	1 tsp salt	oil, for deep-frying

1 Using a sharp knife, slice the eggplants into fairly thin rounds.

2 Place the egg white in a small bowl and beat until light and foamy.

3 Mix together the cornstarch, salt, and seven-spice powder on a large plate.

4 Heat the oil for deep-frying in a large wok.

5 Dip each piece of eggplant into the beaten egg white, then coat in the cornstarch and seven-spice mixture.

6 Deep-fry the coated eggplant slices, in batches, for about 5 minutes, or until pale golden brown and crispy.

7 Transfer the eggplants to absorbent paper towels to drain thoroughly. Transfer the slices to serving plates and serve hot.

COOK'S TIP

The best oil to use for deep-frying is peanut oil which has a high smoke point and mild flavor, so it will neither burn or taint the food. About 2½ cups oil is sufficient.

COOK'S TIP

Thai seven-spice seasoning can be found on the spice shelves of most large supermarkets.

Stir-Fried Bean Curd with Peanut & Chili Sauce

Serves 4

INGREDIENTS

1 pound bean curd, cubed
oil, for frying

SAUCE:
6 tbsp crunchy peanut butter
1 tbsp sweet chili sauce

$^2/_3$ cup coconut milk
1 tbsp tomato paste
$^1/_4$ cup chopped salted peanuts

1 Pat away any moisture from the bean curd, using absorbent paper towels.

2 Heat the oil in a large wok until very hot. Cook the bean curd, in batches, for about 5 minutes, or until golden and crispy. Remove the bean curd with a slotted spoon, transfer to absorbent paper towels and set aside to drain.

3 To make the sauce, mix together the crunchy peanut butter, sweet chili sauce, coconut milk, tomato paste, and chopped peanuts in a bowl. Add a little boiling water if necessary to achieve a smooth consistency.

4 Transfer the crispy fried bean curd to serving plates and serve with the peanut and chili sauce.

COOK'S TIP

Make sure that all of the moisture has been absorbed from the bean curd before frying, otherwise it will not turn crisp.

COOK'S TIP

Cook the peanut and chili sauce in a saucepan over a gentle heat before serving, if desired.

Crispy Seaweed

Serves 4

INGREDIENTS

2¼ pounds bok choy	1 tsp salt
peanut oil, for deep frying	1 tbsp sugar
(about 3¾ cups)	½ cup toasted pine nuts

1 Rinse the bok choy leaves under cold running water, then pat dry thoroughly with absorbent paper towels.

2 Roll each bok choy leaf up, then slice through thinly so that the leaves are finely shredded.

3 Heat the oil in a large wok. Add the shredded leaves and fry for about 30 seconds, or until they shrivel up and become crispy (you may need to do this in about 4 batches).

4 Remove the crispy seaweed from the wok with a slotted spoon and set aside to drain on absorbent paper towels.

5 Transfer the crispy seaweed to a large bowl and toss with the salt, sugar, and pine nuts. Serve immediately.

COOK'S TIP

As a time-saver, you can use a food processor to shred the bok choy finely. Make sure you use only the best leaves; sort through the bok choy and discard any tough, outer leaves, as these will spoil the overall taste and texture of the dish.

VARIATION

Use savoy cabbage instead of the bok choy if it is unavailable, making sure the leaves are well dried before frying.

Spicy Chicken Livers with Bok Choy

Serves 4

INGREDIENTS

12 ounces chicken livers	1 tsp fresh grated ginger	3 tbsp soy sauce
2 tbsp sunflower oil	2 cloves garlic, crushed	1 tsp cornstarch
1 red chili, seeded and finely	2 tbsp tomato ketchup	1 pound bok choy
chopped	3 tbsp sherry	egg noodles, to serve

1 Using a sharp knife, trim the fat from the chicken livers and slice them into small pieces.

2 Heat the oil in a large preheated wok. Add the chicken liver pieces and stir-fry over a high heat for 2–3 minutes.

3 Add the chili, ginger, and garlic and stir-fry for about 1 minute.

4 Mix together the tomato ketchup, sherry, soy sauce, and cornstarch in a small bowl and set aside.

5 Add the bok choy to the wok and stir-fry until it just wilts.

6 Add the reserved tomato ketchup mixture to the wok and cook, stirring to mix, until the juices start to bubble.

7 Transfer to serving bowls and serve hot with noodles.

COOK'S TIP

Fresh ginger root will keep for several weeks in a dry, cool place.

COOK'S TIP

Chicken livers are available fresh or frozen from most supermarkets.

Thai-Style Fish Cakes

Serves 4

INGREDIENTS

1 pound cod fillets, skinned	2 cloves garlic, crushed	¼ cup all-purpose flour
2 tbsp fish sauce	10 lime leaves, very finely chopped	¾ cup fine green beans,
2 red Thai chiles, seeded and very	2 tbsp fresh cilantro, chopped	very finely sliced
finely chopped	1 large egg	peanut oil, for frying

1 Using a sharp knife, roughly cut the cod fillets into bite-size pieces.

2 Place the cod pieces in a food processor, with the fish sauce, chiles, garlic, lime leaves, cilantro, egg and all-purpose flour. Process until finely chopped and turn out into a large mixing bowl.

3 Add the green beans to the cod mixture and combine.

4 Divide the mixture into small balls. Flatten the balls between the palms of your hands to form rounds.

5 Heat a little oil in a preheated wok. Fry the fish cakes on both sides until brown and crispy on the outside.

6 Transfer the fish cakes to serving plates and serve hot.

VARIATION

Almost any kind of fish fillets and seafood can be used in this recipe, try haddock, crab meat, or lobster.

COOK'S TIP

Fish sauce is a salty, brown liquid which is a must for authentic flavor. It is used to salt dishes, but is milder in flavor than soy sauce. It is available from Chinese foodstores or healthfood shops.

Crispy Chili & Peanut Shrimp

Serves 4

INGREDIENTS

1 pound jumbo shrimp, peeled apart from the tails	1 tbsp chili sauce	1¾ ounces fine egg noodles
3 tbsp crunchy peanut butter	10 sheets filo pastry	oil, for frying
	2 tbsp butter, melted	

1 Using a sharp knife, make a small horizontal slit across the back of each shrimp. Press down on the shrimp so that they lie flat.

2 Mix together the peanut butter and chili sauce in a small bowl. Spread a little of the sauce onto each shrimp.

3 Cut each pastry sheet in half and brush one side of each sheet with melted butter.

4 Wrap each shrimp in a piece of pastry, tucking the edges under to enclose the shrimp fully.

5 Place the egg noodles in a bowl, pour over enough boiling water to cover, and let stand for 5 minutes. Drain the noodles thoroughly. Use 2–3 cooked noodles to tie around each shrimp.

6 Heat the oil in a preheated wok. Cook the shrimp for 3–4 minutes, or until golden and crispy.

7 Remove the shrimp with a slotted spoon, transfer to absorbent paper towels and set aside to drain. Transfer to serving plates and serve warm.

COOK'S TIP

When using filo pastry, keep any unused pastry covered to prevent it from drying out.

Shrimp Packets

Serves 4

INGREDIENTS

1 tbsp sunflower oil	½ inch piece of ginger root, peeled and grated	8 sheets filo pastry
1 red bell pepper, seeded and very thinly sliced	8 ounces peeled shrimp	2 tbsp butter
⅓ cup bean sprouts	1 tbsp fish sauce	2 tsp sesame oil
finely grated zest and juice of 1 lime	½ tsp arrowroot	oil, for frying
1 red Thai chili, seeded and very finely chopped	2 tbsp chopped fresh cilantro	scallion tassels, to garnish
		chili sauce, to serve

1 Heat the sunflower oil in a large preheated wok. Add the red bell pepper and bean sprouts and stir-fry for 2 minutes, or until the vegetables have softened.

2 Remove the wok from the heat and toss in the lime zest and juice, red chili, ginger, and shrimp, stirring well.

3 Mix the fish sauce with the arrowroot and stir the mixture into the wok juices. Return the wok to the heat and cook, stirring, for 2 minutes, or until the juices thicken. Toss in the cilantro and mix well.

4 Lay the sheets of filo pastry out on a board. Melt the butter with the sesame oil and brush the pastry with the mixture.

5 Spoon a little of the shrimp filling onto the top of each sheet, fold over each end, and roll up to enclose the filling.

6 Heat the oil in a large wok. Cook the packets, in batches, for 2–3 minutes, or until crisp and golden. Garnish with scallion tassels and serve hot with a chili dipping sauce.

COOK'S TIP

If using cooked shrimp, cook for 1 minute only, otherwise the shrimp will toughen.

Chinese Shrimp Salad

Serves 4

INGREDIENTS

9 ounces fine egg noodles	¾ cup bean sprouts	12 ounces peeled cooked shrimp
3 tbsp sunflower oil	1 ripe mango, sliced	2 tbsp light soy sauce
1 tbsp sesame oil	6 scallions, sliced	1 tbsp sherry
1 tbsp sesame seeds	2¾ ounces radishes, sliced	

1 Place the egg noodles in a large bowl and pour over enough boiling water to cover. Let stand for 10 minutes.

2 Drain the noodles thoroughly and pat away any moisture with absorbent paper towels.

3 Heat the sunflower oil in a large preheated wok. Add the noodles and stir-fry for 5 minutes, tossing frequently.

4 Remove the wok from the heat and add the sesame oil, sesame seeds, and bean sprouts, tossing to mix well.

5 In a separate bowl, mix together the sliced mango, scallions, radishes, shrimp, light soy sauce, and sherry.

6 Toss the shrimp mixture with the noodles or alternatively, arrange the noodles around the edge of a serving plate and pile the shrimp mixture into the center. Serve immediately.

VARIATION

If fresh mango is unavailable, use canned mango slices, rinsed and drained, instead.

Sesame Shrimp Toasts

Serves 4

INGREDIENTS

4 slices medium, thick-sliced white bread	2 cloves garlic, crushed	2 tbsp sesame seeds
8 ounces cooked peeled shrimp	1 tbsp sesame oil	oil, for frying
1 tbsp soy sauce	1 egg	sweet chili sauce, to serve

1 Remove the crusts from the bread, if desired, then set the slices of bread aside until they are required.

2 Place the peeled shrimp, soy sauce, crushed garlic, sesame oil, and egg in a food processor and process until a smooth paste has formed.

3 Spread the shrimp paste evenly over the 4 slices of bread.

4 Sprinkle the sesame seeds over the top of the shrimp mixture and press the seeds down with your hands so that they stick to the mixture.

5 Cut each slice of bread in half and then in half again to form 4 triangles.

6 Heat the oil in a large wok and deep-fry the toasts, sesame seed side up, for 4–5 minutes, or until golden and crispy.

7 Remove the toasts with a slotted spoon, transfer to absorbent paper towels and set aside to drain thoroughly. Serve the shrimp toasts warm with sweet chili sauce for dipping.

VARIATION

Add two chopped scallions to the mixture in step 2 for added flavor and crunch.

Shrimp & Mushroom Omelet

Serves 4

INGREDIENTS

3 tbsp sunflower oil	4 tbsp cornstarch	¾ cup bean sprouts
2 leeks, trimmed and sliced	1 tsp salt	6 eggs
12 ounces raw jumbo shrimp	2⅓ cups sliced mushrooms	deep-fried leeks, to garnish (optional)

1 Heat the sunflower oil in a large preheated wok. Add the sliced leeks and stir-fry for about 3 minutes.

2 Rinse the shrimp under cold running water, drain, and then pat thoroughly dry with absorbent paper towels.

3 Mix together the cornstarch and salt in a large bowl.

4 Add the jumbo shrimp to the cornstarch and salt mixture and toss well to coat them all over.

5 Add the coated shrimp to the wok and stir-fry for 2 minutes, or until the shrimp are almost cooked through.

6 Add the mushrooms and bean sprouts to the wok and stir-fry for a further 2 minutes.

7 Lightly beat the eggs with 3 tablespoons of cold water. Pour the egg mixture into the wok and cook until the egg has just set, carefully turning the omelet over once. Turn the omelet out onto a clean board, divide it into 4 portions, and transfer to warm plates.

COOK'S TIP

If desired, divide the mixture into 4 once the initial cooking has taken place in step 6 and cook 4 individual omelets.

Salt & Pepper Shrimp

Serves 4

INGREDIENTS

2 tsp salt	1 pound peeled raw jumbo shrimp	1 tsp freshly grated ginger
1 tsp black pepper	2 tbsp peanut oil	3 cloves garlic, crushed
2 tsp Szechuan peppercorns	1 red chili, seeded and finely	scallions, sliced, to garnish
1 tsp sugar	chopped	shrimp crackers, to serve

1 Finely grind the salt, black pepper and Szechuan peppercorns in a mortar with a pestle. Mix the salt and pepper mixture with the sugar and set aside until required.

2 Rinse the shrimp under cold running water and pat dry with absorbent paper towels.

3 Heat the oil in a preheated wok. Add the shrimp, chili, ginger, and garlic and stir-fry for 4–5 minutes, or until the shrimp are cooked through and have changed color.

4 Add the salt and pepper mixture to the wok and stir-fry for 1 minute.

5 Transfer to warm serving bowls and garnish with sliced scallion. Serve immediately with shrimp crackers.

COOK'S TIP

Szechuan peppercorns are also known as farchiew. These wild reddish-brown peppercorns from the Szechuan region of China add an aromatic flavor to a dish.

COOK'S TIP

Jumbo shrimp are widely available and are not only colorful and tasty, but they have a meaty texture, too. If cooked jumbo shrimp are used, add them with the salt and pepper mixture in step 4 — if the cooked shrimp are added any earlier they will toughen up and be inedible.

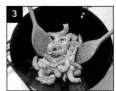

Spring Rolls

Serves 4

INGREDIENTS

6 ounces cooked pork, chopped
2¾ ounces cooked chicken, chopped
1 tsp light soy sauce
1 tsp light brown sugar
1 tsp sesame oil
1 tsp vegetable oil

8 ounces bean sprouts
1 ounce canned bamboo shoots, drained, rinsed, and chopped
1 green bell pepper, seeded and chopped
2 scallions, sliced
1 tsp cornstarch

2 tsp water
vegetable oil, for deep-frying
skins:
1⅛ cups all-purpose flour
5 tbsp cornstarch
2 cups water
3 tbsp vegetable oil

1 Mix the pork, chicken, soy sauce, sugar, and sesame oil. Cover and marinate for 30 minutes.

2 Heat the oil in a preheated wok. Stir-fry the bean sprouts, bamboo shoots, bell pepper, and scallions for 2–3 minutes. Add the meat and the marinade and stir-fry for a further 2–3 minutes.

3 Blend the cornstarch with the water and stir the mixture into the wok. Set aside to cool completely.

4 To make the skins, mix the flour and cornstarch, and gradually stir in the water to make a smooth batter.

5 Heat a small, oiled skillet. Swirl ⅛ of the batter over the base and cook for 2–3 minutes. Repeat. Cover with a damp cloth.

6 Spread out the skins and spoon one-eighth of the filling along the center of each. Brush the edges with water and fold in the sides, then roll up.

7 Heat the oil for deep-frying in a wok until a cube of bread browns in 30 seconds. Cook the spring rolls, in batches, for 2–3 minutes, or until golden and crisp. Remove from the oil and drain on absorbent paper towels. Transfer to a serving dish and serve at once.

Pork Dim Sum

Serves 4

INGREDIENTS

14 ounces ground pork	1 tbsp light soy sauce	1 egg white, lightly beaten
2 scallions, chopped	1 tbsp dry sherry	4½ tsp cornstarch
1¾ ounces canned bamboo shoots, drained, rinsed, and chopped	2 tsp sesame oil	24 wonton wrappers
	2 tsp superfine sugar	

1 Mix together the ground pork, chopped scallions, bamboo shoots, soy sauce, dry sherry, sesame oil, sugar, and beaten egg white in a bowl until well combined.

2 Stir in the cornstarch, mixing thoroughly.

3 Spread out the wonton wrappers on a counter. Place a spoonful of the pork and vegetable mixture in the center of each wonton wrapper and lightly brush the edges of the wrappers with water.

4 Bring the sides of the wrappers together in the center of the filling, pinching firmly together.

5 Line a steamer with a clean, damp dish cloth and arrange the wontons inside. Cover and steam for 5–7 minutes, until cooked through. Serve.

COOK'S TIP

Bamboo steamers are designed to rest on the sloping sides of a wok above the water. They are available in a range of sizes.

VARIATION

Use shrimp, ground chicken, or crab meat for the filling, with other vegetables, such as chopped carrot, and flavorings, such as chili or ginger, if desired.

Crispy Crab Wontons

Serves 4

INGREDIENTS

6 ounces white crab meat, flaked	1 scallion, chopped	24 wonton wrappers
1¾ ounces canned water	1 tbsp cornstarch	vegetable oil, for deep-frying
chestnuts, drained, rinsed,	1 tsp dry sherry	sliced lime, to garnish
and chopped	1 tsp light soy sauce	
1 small fresh red chili, chopped	½ tsp lime juice	

1 To make the filling, mix together the crab meat, water chestnuts, chili, scallion, cornstarch, sherry, soy sauce, and lime juice in a bowl.

2 Spread out the wonton wrappers on a counter and spoon one portion of the crab meat filling into the center of each wonton wrapper.

3 Dampen the edges of the wonton wrappers with a little water and fold them in half to form triangles. Fold the two pointed ends in toward the center, moisten with a little water to secure, and then pinch together to seal.

4 Heat the oil for deep-frying in a wok or deep-fryer until a cube of bread browns in 30 seconds. Fry the wontons, in batches, for 2–3 minutes, until golden brown and crisp. Remove the wontons from the oil with a slotted spoon and drain on paper towels.

5 Transfer the wontons to a serving dish, garnish with slices of lime, and serve hot.

COOK'S TIP

Wonton wrappers, available from Chinese grocery stores, are paper-thin squares made from wheat flour and egg. They can be easily damaged, so handle them carefully. Make sure that the wontons are sealed well before deep-frying to prevent the filling from coming out and the wontons unwrapping.

Pot Sticker Dumplings

Serves 4

INGREDIENTS

DUMPLINGS:
1½ cups all-purpose flour
pinch of salt
3 tbsp vegetable oil
6–8 tbsp boiling water
oil, for deep-frying
sliced scallions and chives, to
    garnish

FILLING:
5½ ounces lean chicken, very
    finely chopped
1 ounce canned bamboo shoots,
    drained and chopped
2 scallions, finely chopped
½ small red bell pepper, seeded
    and finely chopped

½ tsp Chinese curry powder
1 tbsp light soy sauce
1 tsp superfine sugar
1 tsp sesame oil

1 To make the dumplings, mix together the flour and salt in a bowl. Make a well in the center, add the oil and water, and mix well to form a soft dough. Knead the dough on a lightly floured surface, wrap in plastic wrap, and let stand for 30 minutes.

2 Meanwhile, put all the filling ingredients in a large bowl and mix thoroughly.

3 Divide the dough into 12 equal-size pieces and roll each piece into a 5-inch round. Spoon a portion of the filling onto one half of each round.

4 Fold the dough over the filling to form a "turnover," pressing the edges together to seal.

5 Pour a little oil into a heavy-based skillet and cook the dumplings, in batches, until slightly crisp.

6 Drain the oil from the skillet. Return all of the dumplings to the skillet and add about ½ cup water. Cover and steam for 5 minutes, or until the dumplings are cooked through. Remove with a slotted spoon and transfer to a serving dish. Garnish and serve with soy or hoisin sauce.

Pancake Rolls

Serves 4

INGREDIENTS

4 tsp vegetable oil
1–2 garlic cloves, crushed
8 ounces ground pork
8 ounces bok choy, shredded

4½ tsp light soy sauce
½ tsp sesame oil
8 spring roll skins, 10 inches
   square, thawed if frozen

oil, for deep-frying
chili sauce (see Cook's Tip,
   below), to serve

1 Heat the vegetable oil in a preheated wok. Add the garlic and stir-fry for 30 seconds. Add the pork and stir-fry for about 2–3 minutes, until just becoming lightly colored.

2 Add the shredded bok choy, soy sauce, and sesame oil to the wok and stir-fry for 2–3 minutes. Remove from the heat and set aside to cool.

3 Spread out the spring roll skins on a counter and spoon 2 tablespoons of the pork mixture along one edge of each. Roll the skin over once and fold in the sides. Roll up completely to make a sausage shape, brushing the edges with a little water to seal. If you have time, set the pancake rolls aside for 10 minutes to seal firmly.

4 Heat the oil for deep-frying in a wok until almost smoking. Reduce the heat slightly and fry the pancake rolls, in batches if necessary, for 3–4 minutes, until golden brown. Remove from the oil with a slotted spoon and drain on paper towels. Serve at once with chili sauce.

COOK'S TIP

To make chili sauce, heat ¼ cup superfine sugar, ¼ cup rice vinegar, and 2 tablespoons water in a small saucepan, stirring until the sugar has dissolved. Bring the mixture to a boil and boil rapidly until a light syrup forms. Remove the pan from the heat and stir in 2 finely chopped, fresh red chiles. Let the sauce cool before serving. If you prefer a milder dipping sauce, seed the chiles before chopping them.

Sweet & Sour Fried Shrimp

Serves 4

INGREDIENTS

16 large raw shrimp, peeled
1 tsp grated fresh ginger root
1 garlic clove, crushed
2 scallions, sliced
2 tbsp dry sherry
2 tsp sesame oil
1 tbsp light soy sauce
vegetable oil, for deep-frying
shredded scallion,
   to garnish

BATTER:
4 egg whites
4 tbsp cornstarch
2 tbsp all-purpose flour

SAUCE:
2 tbsp tomato paste
3 tbsp white wine vinegar
4 tsp light soy sauce
2 tbsp lemon juice

3 tbsp light brown sugar
1 green bell pepper, seeded and
   cut into thin matchsticks
1/2 tsp chili sauce
1 1/4 cups vegetable stock
2 tsp cornstarch

1 Using tweezers, devein the shrimp, then flatten them with a large knife.

2 Place the shrimp in a shallow dish and add the ginger, garlic, scallions, sherry, sesame oil, and soy sauce. Cover and marinate 30 minutes.

3 Make the batter by beating the egg whites until thick. Fold in the cornstarch and flour to form a light batter.

4 Place all the sauce ingredients in a pan and bring to a boil. Reduce the heat and simmer for 10 minutes.

5 Remove the shrimp from the marinade and dip them into the batter to coat.

6 Heat the oil until almost smoking. Reduce the heat and fry the shrimp for about 3–4 minutes, until crisp and golden brown. Serve with the sauce.

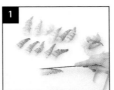

Shrimp Rice Paper Packets

Serves 4

INGREDIENTS

1 egg white
2 tsp cornstarch
2 tsp dry sherry
1 tsp superfine sugar
2 tsp hoisin sauce

8 ounces peeled, cooked shrimp
4 scallions, sliced
1 ounce canned water chestnuts,
    drained, rinsed, and chopped

8 Chinese rice paper wrappers
vegetable oil, for deep-frying
hoisin sauce or plum sauce,
    to serve

1 Lightly beat the egg white, then mix in the cornstarch, dry sherry, superfine sugar, and hoisin sauce. Add the shrimp, sliced scallions, and water chestnuts, mixing together thoroughly.

2 Soften the rice papers by dipping them in a bowl of water one at a time. Spread them out on a counter.

3 Spoon a little of the shrimp mixture into the center of each rice paper and wrap the paper around the filling to make a secure packet.

4 Heat the oil in a wok until it is almost smoking. Reduce the heat slightly, add the packets, in batches if necessary, and deep-fry for 4–5 minutes, until crisp. Remove from the oil with a slotted spoon and drain on absorbent paper towels.

5 Transfer the packets to a warm serving dish and serve immediately with a little hoisin or plum sauce.

COOK'S TIP

Use this filling inside wonton wrappers if the rice paper wrappers are unavailable.

Crab Ravioli

Serves 4

INGREDIENTS

1 pound crab meat (fresh or canned and drained)	1 ounce bean sprouts, roughly chopped	2 tbsp peanut oil
1/2 red bell pepper, seeded and finely diced	1 tbsp light soy sauce	1 tsp sesame oil
4 1/2 ounces Chinese cabbage, shredded	1 tsp lime juice	salt and pepper
	16 wonton wrappers	
	1 small egg, beaten	

1 Mix together the crab meat, bell pepper, Chinese cabbage, bean sprouts, soy sauce, and lime juice in a bowl. Season and let stand for 15 minutes, stirring the mixture occasionally.

2 Spread out the wonton wrappers on a counter. Spoon a little of the crab meat mixture into the center of each wrapper, dividing it equally among them.

3 Brush the edges of the wrappers with the beaten egg and fold in half, pushing out any air. Press the edges together with your fingers to seal tightly.

4 Heat the peanut oil in a preheated wok or heavy-based skillet. Fry the ravioli, in batches, for 3–4 minutes, turning until browned. Remove with a slotted spoon and drain thoroughly on paper towels.

5 Heat the remaining filling in the wok or skillet over a gentle heat until hot. Serve the ravioli with the hot filling and sprinkled with sesame oil.

COOK'S TIP

Make sure that the edges of the ravioli are sealed well and that all of the air is pressed out to prevent them from opening during cooking.

Spareribs

Serves 4

INGREDIENTS

2 pounds pork spareribs

2 tbsp dark soy sauce

3 tbsp hoisin sauce

1 tbsp Chinese rice wine or dry
sherry

pinch of Chinese five-spice powder

2 tsp dark brown sugar

¼ tsp chili sauce

2 garlic cloves, crushed

cilantro sprigs, to garnish
(optional)

1 Cut the spareribs into separate pieces if they are joined together. If desired, you can chop them into 2-inch lengths.

2 Mix together the soy sauce, hoisin sauce, Chinese rice wine or sherry, Chinese five-spice powder, dark brown sugar, chili sauce, and garlic in a large bowl.

3 Place the ribs in a shallow dish and pour the mixture over them, turning to make sure they are well coated. Cover and marinate in the refrigerator, turning the ribs from time to time, for at least 1 hour.

4 Remove the ribs from the marinade and arrange them in a single layer on a wire rack placed over a roasting pan half filled with warm water. Brush with the marinade, reserving the remainder.

5 Cook in a preheated oven at 350°F for 30 minutes. Remove the roasting pan from the oven and turn the ribs over. Brush with the remaining marinade and return to the oven for a further 30 minutes, or until cooked through. Transfer to a warm serving dish, garnish with the cilantro sprigs (if using), and serve the ribs immediately.

COOK'S TIP

Add more hot water to the roasting pan during cooking if required. Do not allow it to dry out, as the water steams the ribs and aids in their cooking.

Honeyed Chicken Wings

Serves 4

INGREDIENTS

1 pound chicken wings
2 tbsp peanut oil
2 tbsp light soy sauce
2 tbsp hoisin sauce
2 tbsp clear honey
2 garlic cloves, crushed
1 tsp sesame seeds

MARINADE:
1 dried red chili
$^1/_2$–1 tsp chili powder
$^1/_2$–1 tsp ground ginger
finely grated rind of 1 lime

1 To make the marinade, crush the dried chili in a mortar with a pestle. Mix together the crushed dried chili, chili powder, ground ginger, and lime rind in a small mixing bowl.

2 Thoroughly rub the spice mixture into the chicken wings with your fingertips. Set aside for at least 2 hours to allow the flavors to penetrate the chicken wings.

3 Heat the peanut oil in a preheated wok.

4 Add the chicken wings and fry, turning frequently, for 10–12 minutes, until golden and crisp. Drain off any excess oil.

5 Add the soy sauce, hoisin sauce, honey, garlic, and sesame seeds to the wok, turning the chickens wings to coat them with the mixture.

6 Reduce the heat and cook for 20–25 minutes, turning the chicken wings frequently, until completely cooked through. Serve hot.

COOK'S TIP

Make the dish in advance and freeze the chicken wings. Thaw thoroughly, cover with foil, and heat through in a moderate oven.

Steamed Duck Buns

Serves 4

INGREDIENTS

DUMPLING DOUGH:
$2^2/3$ cups all-purpose flour
$1/2$ ounce dried yeast
1 tsp superfine sugar
2 tbsp warm water
$3/4$ cup warm milk

FILLING:
$10^1/2$ ounces duck breast
1 tbsp light brown sugar
1 tbsp light soy sauce
2 tbsp clear honey
1 tbsp hoisin sauce

1 tbsp vegetable oil
1 leek, finely chopped
1 garlic clove, crushed
$1/2$-inch piece fresh ginger
    root, grated

1 Place the duck breast in a large bowl. Mix together the sugar, soy sauce, honey, and hoisin sauce. Pour the mixture over the duck and marinate for 20 minutes.

2 Remove the duck from the marinade and cook on a rack set over a roasting pan in a preheated oven at 400°F for 35–40 minutes, or until cooked through. Let cool, remove the meat from the bones, and cut into small cubes.

3 Heat the oil in a wok and fry the leek, garlic, and ginger for 3 minutes. Mix with the duck meat.

4 Sift the flour into a large bowl. Mix the yeast, sugar, and water in a separate bowl and leave in a warm place for 15 minutes. Pour the yeast mixture into the flour, together with the warm milk, mixing to form a firm dough.

5 Knead the dough on a floured surface for 5 minutes. Roll into a sausage shape, 1 inch in diameter. Cut into 16 pieces, cover, and let stand for 20–25 minutes.

6 Flatten the dough pieces into 4-inch rounds. Place a spoonful of filling in the center of each, draw up the sides to form a "moneybag," and twist to seal.

7 Place the dumplings on a clean dish cloth in the base of a steamer, cover, and steam for 20 minutes.

Spinach Meatballs

Serves 4

INGREDIENTS

4½ ounces pork
1 small egg
½-inch piece fresh ginger
    root, chopped
1 small onion, finely chopped
1 tbsp boiling water

1 ounce canned bamboo shoots,
    drained, rinsed, and chopped
2 slices smoked ham, chopped
2 tsp cornstarch
1 pound fresh spinach
2 tsp sesame seeds

SAUCE:
⅔ cup vegetable stock
½ tsp cornstarch
1 tsp cold water
1 tsp light soy sauce
½ tsp sesame oil
1 tbsp chopped chives

1 Grind the pork very finely in a food processor or meat grinder. Lightly beat the egg in a bowl and stir into the pork.

2 Put the ginger andonion in a separate bowl, add the boiling water, and let stand for 5 minutes. Drain and add to the pork mixture, together with the bamboo shoots, ham and cornstarch. Mix and roll into 12 balls between the palms of your hands.

3 Wash the spinach and remove the stalks. Blanch in boiling water for 10 seconds and drain well, pressing out as much moisture as possible. Slice the spinach into very thin strips, then mix with the sesame seeds. Spread out the mixture in a shallow baking pan. Roll the meatballs in the mixture to coat.

4 Place the meatballs on a heatproof plate in the base of a steamer. Cover and steam for 8–10 minutes, until cooked through and tender.

5 Meanwhile, make the sauce. Put the stock in a saucepan and bring to a boil. Mix together the cornstarch and water to a smooth paste and stir it into the stock. Stir in the soy sauce, sesame oil, and chives. Transfer the cooked meatballs to a warm plate and serve with the sauce.

Steamed Cabbage Rolls

Serves 4

INGREDIENTS

8 cabbage leaves, trimmed
8 ounces skinless, boneless
   chicken
6 ounces peeled raw or
   cooked shrimp

1 tsp cornstarch
1/2 tsp chili powder
1 egg, lightly beaten
1 tbsp vegetable oil
1 leek, sliced

1 garlic clove, thinly sliced
sliced fresh red chili, to garnish

1 Bring a large saucepan of water to a boil. Blanch the cabbage leaves for 2 minutes. Drain, rinse under cold water, and drain again. Pat completely dry with paper towels and spread out on a counter.

2 Put the chicken and shrimp into a food processor and process until finely ground. Alternatively, grind them together in a meat grinder. Transfer the chicken mixture to a large bowl and add the cornstarch, chili powder, and egg, mixing together thoroughly.

3 Place 2 tablespoons of the chicken and shrimp mixture toward one end of each cabbage leaf. Fold the sides of the cabbage leaf around the filling and roll up to form a tight packet.

4 Arrange the packets, seam side down, in a single layer on a heatproof plate and cook in a steamer for 10 minutes, or until cooked through.

5 Meanwhile, heat the vegetable oil in a preheated wok. Add the

leek and garlic and sauté for 1–2 minutes.

6 Transfer the cabbage packets to warmed individual serving plates and garnish with red chili slices. Serve with the leek and garlic sauté.

COOK'S TIP

Use Chinese cabbage or Savoy cabbage for this recipe, choosing leaves of a similar size for the packets.

Chinese Omelet

Serves 4

INGREDIENTS

8 eggs
2 cups cooked chicken, shredded
12 jumbo shrimp, peeled and
    deveined

2 tbsp chopped chives
2 tsp light soy sauce
dash of chili sauce
2 tbsp vegetable oil

1 Lightly beat the eggs in a large mixing bowl.

2 Add the shredded chicken and jumbo shrimp to the eggs, mixing well.

3 Stir in the chopped chives, soy sauce, and chili sauce, mixing well.

4 Heat the oil in a large skillet over a medium heat and add the egg mixture, tilting the skillet to coat the base completely. Cook over a medium heat, gently stirring the omelet with a fork occasionally, until the surface is just set and the underside is a golden brown color.

5 When the omelet is set, slide it out of the skillet with a spatula.

6 Cut the omelet into squares or slices to serve.

VARIATION

You could add extra flavor to the omelet by stirring in 3 tablespoons finely chopped fresh cilantro or 1 teaspoon sesame seeds with the chives in step 3.

COOK'S TIP

Add peas or other vegetables to the omelet and serve as a main course for 2 people.

Thai-Style Chicken Skewers

Serves 4

INGREDIENTS

4 skinless, boneless chicken
  breasts
1 onion, peeled and cut into
  wedges
1 large red bell pepper, seeded

1 large yellow bell pepper seeded
12 kaffir lime leaves
2 tbsp sunflower oil
2 tbsp lime juice
tomato halves, to serve

MARINADE:
1 tbsp Thai red curry paste
²/₃ cup canned coconut milk

1 To make the marinade, place the red curry paste in a small pan over medium heat and cook for 1 minute. Add half of the coconut milk to the pan and bring the mixture to a boil. Boil for 2–3 minutes, until the liquid has reduced by about two-thirds.

2 Remove the pan from the heat and stir in the remaining coconut milk. Set aside to cool.

3 Cut the chicken into 1-inch pieces. Stir the chicken into the cold marinade, cover, and chill for at least 2 hours.

4 Cut the onion into wedges and the bell peppers into 1-inch pieces.

5 Remove the chicken pieces from the marinade and thread them onto skewers, alternating the chicken with the vegetables and lime leaves.

6 Combine the oil and lime juice in a small bowl and brush the mixture over the kabobs. Broil the skewers over hot coals, turning and basting frequently with the oil and lime mixture, for 10–15 minutes, until the chicken is cooked through. Broil the tomato halves on the barbecue and serve with the chicken skewers.

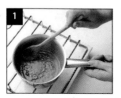

Sesame Chicken Brochettes with Cranberry Sauce

Makes 8

INGREDIENTS

4 skinless, boneless chicken breasts	salt and pepper	SAUCE:
4 tbsp dry white wine		1½ cups cranberries
1 tbsp light brown sugar	TO SERVE:	⅔ cup cranberry juice drink
2 tbsp sunflower oil	boiled new potatoes	2 tbsp light muscovado sugar
6½ tbsp sesame seeds	salad greens	

1 Cut the chicken into 1-inch pieces. Stir together the wine, sugar, oil, and salt and pepper to taste in a large bowl. Add the chicken and toss to coat. Marinate in the refrigerator for at least 30 minutes, turning the chicken occasionally.

2 To make the sauce, place the ingredients in a small saucepan and bring slowly to a boil, stirring. Simmer gently for 5–10 minutes, until the cranberries are soft. Taste and add extra sugar if desired. Keep warm or chill, as required.

3 Remove the chicken pieces from the marinade with a slotted spoon. Thread the chicken pieces onto 8 skewers, spacing them slightly apart to ensure even cooking.

4 Broil on an oiled rack over hot coals for 4–5 minutes on each side, until just cooked. Brush several times with the marinade during cooking.

5 Remove the chicken skewers from the rack and roll in the sesame seeds. Return to the barbecue and cook for about 1 minute on each side or until the sesame seeds are toasted. Serve with the cranberry sauce, new potatoes, and fresh salad greens.

Meat & Poultry

Meat is expensive in Far Eastern countries and is eaten in smaller proportions than in the Western world. However, meat is used to its full potential – it is marinated or spiced and combined with other delicious native flavourings to create a wide array of delicious dishes.

In Malaysia, a wide variety of spicy meats is offered, reflecting the many ethnic origins of the population. Chicken is the most frequently used poultry in Malaysia – it is marinated, grilled and stir-fried or cooked in the wok as delicious curries and stews.

In China, poultry, lamb, beef and pork are stir-fried or steamed in the wok and combined with sauces and seasonings such as soy, black bean and oyster sauce, and in Japan where a smaller amount of meat is consumed, it is generally marinated and quickly stir-fried in a wok or simmered in miso stock.

The use of meat in Thailand is similar, but it is leaner and has more flavour due to 'free-range' rearing. Meats differ slightly in that beef is probably taken from the buffalo, and lamb on the menu may often be goat, or kid goat.

Stir-Fried Ginger Chicken

Serves 4

INGREDIENTS

2 tbsp sunflower oil	12 ounces boneless skinless	1 tbsp tomato paste
1 onion, sliced	chicken breasts	1 tbsp sugar
6 ounces carrots, cut into thin	2 tbsp ginger root, peeled and	½ cup orange juice
sticks	grated	1 tsp cornstarch
1 clove garlic, crushed	1 tsp ground ginger	1 orange, peeled and segmented
	4 tbsp sweet sherry	fresh snipped chives, to garnish

1 Heat the oil in a large preheated wok. Add the onion, carrots, and garlic and stir-fry over a high heat for 3 minutes, or until the vegetables begin to soften.

2 Using a sharp knife, slice the chicken into thin strips. Add the chicken to the wok, together with the ginger root and ground ginger. Stir-fry for a further 10 minutes, or until the chicken is well cooked through and golden in color.

3 Mix together the sherry, tomato paste, sugar, orange juice, and cornstarch to a smooth paste in a bowl. Stir the mixture into the wok and heat through until the mixture bubbles and the juices start to thicken.

4 Add the orange segments and carefully toss to mix.

5 Transfer the stir-fried chicken to warm serving bowls and garnish with freshly snipped chives. Serve immediately.

COOK'S TIP

Make sure that you do not continue cooking the dish once the orange segments have been added in step 4, otherwise they will break up.

Chicken, Collard Green, & Yellow Bean Stir-Fry

Serves 4

INGREDIENTS

2 tbsp sunflower oil

1 pound skinless, boneless
chicken breasts

2 cloves garlic, crushed

1 green bell pepper

1½ cups snow peas

6 scallions, sliced, plus extra
to garnish

8 ounces collard greens or
cabbage, shredded

5¾ ounce jar yellow bean sauce

3 tbsp roasted cashew nuts

1 Heat the sunflower oil in a large preheated wok.

2 Using a sharp knife, slice the chicken into thin strips.

3 Add the chicken to the wok, together with the garlic. Stir-fry for about 5 minutes, or until the chicken is sealed on all sides and beginning to turn golden.

4 Using a sharp knife, seed the green bell pepper and cut the flesh into thin strips.

5 Add the snow peas, scallions, green bell pepper strips, and collard greens or cabbage to the wok. Stir-fry for a further 5 minutes, or until the vegetables are just tender.

6 Stir in the yellow bean sauce and heat through for about 2 minutes, or until the mixture starts to bubble.

7 Generously scatter the stir-fry with the roasted cashew nuts.

8 Transfer the chicken, collard green, and yellow bean stir-fry to warm serving plates and garnish with extra scallions, if desired. Serve the stir-fry immediately.

COOK'S TIP

Do not add salted cashew nuts to this dish, otherwise, combined with the slightly salty sauce, the dish will be very salty indeed.

Chicken, Bell Pepper, & Orange Stir-Fry

Serves 4

INGREDIENTS

3 tbsp sunflower oil

12 ounces skinless, boneless
    chicken thighs, cut into
    thin strips

1 onion, sliced

1 clove garlic, crushed

1 red bell pepper, seeded and
    sliced

1¼ cups snow peas

4 tbsp light soy sauce

4 tbsp sherry

1 tbsp tomato paste

finely grated rind and juice
    of 1 orange

1 tsp cornstarch

2 oranges

½ cup bean sprouts

cooked rice or noodles, to serve

1 Heat the sunflower oil in a large preheated wok.

2 Add the strips of chicken to the wok and stir-fry for 2–3 minutes, or until sealed on all sides.

3 Add the sliced onion, garlic, bell pepper and snow peas to the wok. Stir-fry the mixture for a further 5 minutes, or until the vegetables are just becoming tender and the chicken is completely cooked through and golden brown.

4 Mix together the soy sauce, sherry, tomato paste, orange rind and juice, and the cornstarch to a smooth paste.

5 Add the mixture to the wok and cook, stirring, until the juices start to thicken.

6 Using a sharp knife, peel and segment the oranges.

7 Add the orange segments and bean sprouts to the mixture in the wok and heat through for a 2 minutes.

8 Transfer the stir-fry to serving plates and serve at once with rice or noodles.

COOK'S TIP

Bean sprouts are sprouting mung beans and are a regular ingredient in Chinese cooking. They require very little cooking and may even be eaten raw, if desired.

Coconut Chicken Curry

Serves 4

INGREDIENTS
---

2 tbsp sunflower oil or 2 tbsp ghee
1 pound boneless, skinless chicken
   thighs or breasts
1 cup okra
1 large onion, sliced
2 cloves garlic, crushed
3 tbsp mild curry paste
2¼ cups chicken stock

1 tbsp fresh lemon juice
½ cup creamed coconut
1¼ cups fresh or canned
   pineapple, cubes
⅔ cup thick, unsweetened
   yogurt
2 tbsp chopped fresh cilantro
freshly boiled rice, to serve

TO GARNISH:
lemon wedges
fresh cilantro sprigs

1 Heat the sunflower oil or ghee in a large preheated wok.

2 Using a sharp knife, cut the chicken into bite-size pieces. Add the chicken to the wok and cook, stirring frequently, until evenly browned.

3 Using a sharp knife, trim the okra.

4 Add the onion, garlic, and okra to the wok and cook for a further 2–3 minutes, stirring constantly.

5 Mix the curry paste with the chicken stock and lemon juice and pour the mixture into the wok. Bring to a boil, cover, and simmer for 30 minutes.

6 Coarsely grate the creamed coconut, stir it into the curry, and cook for about 5 minutes – the creamed coconut will help to thicken the juices.

7 Add the pineapple, yogurt, and cilantro and heat through for 2 minutes, stirring.

8 Garnish and serve hot with boiled rice.

COOK'S TIP

Score around the top of the okra with a knife before cooking to release the sticky glue-like substance which is bitter in taste.

Sweet & Sour Chicken with Mango

Serves 4

INGREDIENTS

1 tbsp sunflower oil	8 ounces leeks, shredded	2 tbsp clear honey
6 skinless, boneless chicken thighs	½ cup bean sprouts	2 tbsp tomato ketchup
1 ripe mango	⅔ cup mango juice	1 tsp cornstarch
2 cloves garlic, crushed	1 tbsp white wine vinegar	

1 Heat the sunflower oil in a large preheated wok.

2 Using a sharp knife, cut the chicken into bite-size cubes.

3 Add the chicken to the wok and stir-fry over a high heat for 10 minutes, tossing frequently, until the chicken is cooked through and golden in color.

4 Meanwhile, peel and slice the mango.

5 Add the garlic, leeks, mango, and bean sprouts to the wok and stir-fry for a further 2–3 minutes, or until softened.

6 Thoroughly mix together the mango juice, white wine vinegar, clear honey, and tomato ketchup with the cornstarch to make a smooth paste.

7 Pour the mango juice and cornstarch mixture into the wok and stir-fry for a further 2 minutes, or until the juices start to thicken.

8 Transfer to a warm serving dish and serve immediately.

COOK'S TIP

Mango juice is available in jars from most supermarkets and is quite thick and sweet. If unavailable, purée and strain a ripe mango and add a little water to make up the required quantity.

Chicken Stir-Fry with Cumin Seeds & Trio of Bell Peppers

Serves 4

INGREDIENTS

1 pound boneless, skinless chicken breasts	1 red chili, seeded and sliced	½ cup bean sprouts
2 tbsp sunflower oil	1 red bell pepper, seeded and sliced	12 ounces bok choy or other greens
1 clove garlic, crushed	1 green bell pepper, seeded and sliced	2 tbsp sweet chili sauce
1 tbsp cumin seeds	1 yellow bell pepper, seeded and sliced	3 tbsp light soy sauce
1 tbsp grated fresh ginger root		deep-fried crispy ginger, to garnish (see Cook's Tip)

1 Using a sharp knife, slice the chicken breasts into thin strips.

2 Heat the oil in a large preheated wok.

3 Add the chicken to the wok and stir-fry for 5 minutes.

4 Add the garlic, cumin seeds, ginger, and chili to the wok, stirring to mix.

5 Add all the bell peppers to the wok and stir-fry for a further 5 minutes.

6 Toss in the bean sprouts and bok choy, together with the sweet chili sauce and soy sauce and continue to cook until the bok choy leaves start to wilt.

7 Transfer to warm serving bowls and garnish with deep-fried ginger (see Cook's Tip).

COOK'S TIP

To make the deep-fried ginger garnish, peel and thinly slice a large piece of ginger root, using a sharp knife. Carefully lower the slices of ginger into a wok or small pan of hot oil and cook for about 30 seconds. Remove the deep-fried ginger with a slotted spoon, transfer to absorbent paper towels and drain thoroughly.

Stir-Fried Chicken with Lemon & Sesame Seeds

Serves 4

INGREDIENTS

4 boneless, skinless chicken breasts	1 onion, sliced	3 tbsp lemon curd
1 egg white	1 tbsp demerara sugar	7 ounce can water chestnuts
2 tbsp sesame seeds	finely grated zest and juice of	lemon zest, to garnish
2 tbsp vegetable oil	1 lemon	

1 Place the chicken breasts between 2 sheets of plastic wrap and pound with a rolling pin to flatten. Slice the chicken into thin strips.

2 Beat the egg white until it is light and foamy.

3 Dip the chicken strips into the egg white, then into the sesame seeds until coated evenly.

4 Heat the oil in a large preheated wok.

5 Add the onion to the wok and stir-fry for 2 minutes, or until just softened.

6 Add the sesame-coated chicken to the wok and continue stir-frying for 5 minutes, or until the chicken turns golden.

7 Mix together the sugar, lemon zest, lemon juice, and the lemon curd and add the mixture to the wok. Allow the lemon mixture to bubble slightly without stirring.

8 Drain the water chestnuts and slice them thinly, using a sharp knife. Add the water chestnuts to the wok and heat through for 2 minutes. Transfer to serving bowls, garnish with lemon zest, and serve hot.

COOK'S TIP

Water chestnuts are commonly added to Chinese recipes for their crunchy texture, as they do not have a great deal of flavor.

Thai Red Chicken with Cherry Tomatoes

Serves 4

INGREDIENTS

1 tbsp sunflower oil
1 pound boneless, skinless chicken
2 cloves garlic, crushed
2 tbsp Thai red curry paste

2 tbsp fresh grated galangal or
   ginger root
1 tbsp tamarind paste
4 lime leaves
8 ounces sweet potato

2½ cups coconut milk
8 ounces cherry tomatoes, halved
3 tbsp chopped fresh cilantro
cooked jasmine or Thai fragrant
   rice, to serve

---

1 Heat the sunflower oil in a large preheated wok.

2 Thinly slice the chicken. Add the chicken to the wok and stir-fry for 5 minutes.

3 Add the garlic, curry paste, galangal or ginger root, tamarind, and lime leaves to the wok and stir-fry for 1 minute.

4 Using a sharp knife, peel and dice the sweet potato.

5 Add the coconut milk and sweet potato to the mixture in the wok and bring to a boil. Allow to bubble over a medium heat for 20 minutes, or until the juices start to thicken and reduce.

6 Add the cherry tomatoes and cilantro to the curry and cook for a further 5 minutes, stirring occasionally. Transfer to warm serving plates and serve hot with cooked jasmine or Thai fragrant rice.

COOK'S TIP

Galangal is a spice very similar to ginger and is used to replace the latter in Thai cuisine. It can be bought fresh from Chinese foodstores, but is also available dried and as a powder. The fresh root, which is not as pungent as ginger, needs to be peeled before use.

Peppered Chicken Stir-Fried with Sugar Snap Peas

Serves 4

INGREDIENTS

2 tbsp tomato ketchup

2 tbsp soy sauce

1 pound boneless, skinless chicken breasts

2 tbsp crushed mixed peppercorns

2 tbsp sunflower oil

1 red bell pepper

1 green bell pepper

2 1/2 cups sugar snap peas

2 tbsp oyster sauce

1 Mix the tomato ketchup with the soy sauce in a bowl.

2 Using a sharp knife, slice the chicken into thin strips. Toss the chicken in the tomato ketchup and soy sauce mixture.

3 Sprinkle the crushed peppercorns onto a plate. Dip the coated chicken in the peppercorns until evenly coated.

4 Heat the sunflower oil in a preheated wok.

5 Add the chicken to the wok and stir-fry for 5 minutes.

6 Seed and slice the red and green bell peppers.

7 Add the bell peppers to the wok, together with the sugar snap peas and stir-fry for a further 5 minutes.

8 Add the oyster sauce and allow to bubble for 2 minutes. Transfer to warm serving bowls and serve immediately.

VARIATION

You could use snow peas instead of sugar snap peas, if desired.

Honey & Soy Stir-Fried Chicken with Bean Sprouts

Serves 4

INGREDIENTS

2 tbsp clear honey	1 clove garlic, crushed	1 cup baby corn cobs, halved
3 tbsp light soy sauce	8 chicken thighs	8 scallions, sliced
1 tsp Chinese five-spice powder	1 tbsp sunflower oil	3/4 cup bean sprouts
1 tbsp sweet sherry	1 fresh red chili	

1 Mix together the honey, soy sauce, Chinese five-spice powder, sherry, and garlic in a large bowl.

2 Using a sharp knife, make 3 slashes in the skin of each chicken thigh. Brush the honey and soy marinade over the chicken thighs, cover and set aside for at least 30 minutes.

3 Heat the oil in a large preheated wok.

4 Add the chicken to the wok and cook over a fairly high heat for 12–15 minutes, or until the chicken browns and the skin begins to turn crisp. Remove the chicken with a slotted spoon.

5 Using a sharp knife, seed and very finely chop the chili.

6 Add the chili, corn cobs, scallions, and bean sprouts to the wok and stir-fry for about 5 minutes.

7 Return the chicken to the wok and mix all the ingredients together until completely heated through.

8 Transfer to serving plates and serve immediately.

COOK'S TIP

Chinese five-spice powder can be found in most large supermarkets and is a blend of aromatic spices.

Stir-Fried Chicken with Cashew Nuts & Yellow Bean Sauce

Serves 4

INGREDIENTS

1 pound boneless chicken breasts	2¼ cups sliced flat mushrooms	fresh cilantro, to garnish
2 tbsp vegetable oil	1 cup cashew nuts	egg fried rice or plain boiled rice,
1 red onion, sliced	2¾ ounce jar yellow bean sauce	to serve

1 Using a sharp knife, remove the excess skin from the chicken breasts, if desired. Cut the chicken into small, bite-size chunks.

2 Heat the vegetable oil in a preheated wok.

3 Add the chicken to the wok and stir-fry for 5 minutes.

4 Add the red onion and mushrooms to the wok and continue to stir-fry for a further 5 minutes.

5 Place the cashew nuts on a cookie sheet and toast under a preheated broiler until just browning – this brings out their flavor and aroma.

6 Toss the toasted cashew nuts into the wok, together with the yellow bean sauce. Allow the sauce to bubble for 2–3 minutes.

7 Transfer the stir-fry to warm serving bowls and garnish with fresh cilantro. Serve hot with egg fried rice or plain boiled rice, if you wish.

COOK'S TIP

Chicken thighs could be used instead of the chicken breasts for a more economical dish.

Stir-Fried Chicken with Chili & Crispy Basil

Serves 4

INGREDIENTS

8 chicken drumsticks	1–2 medium carrots, cut into	oil, for frying
2 tbsp soy sauce	thin sticks	about 50 fresh basil leaves
1 tbsp sunflower oil	6 celery stalks, cut into sticks	
1 red chili	3 tbsp sweet chili sauce	

1 Remove the skin from the chicken drumsticks, if desired. Make 3 slashes in each drumstick. Brush the drumsticks with the soy sauce.

2 Heat the oil in a preheated wok and fry the drumsticks for 20 minutes, turning frequently, until they are cooked through.

3 Seed and finely chop the chili. Add the chili, carrots, and celery to the wok and cook for a further 5 minutes. Stir in the chili

sauce, cover, and allow to bubble gently while preparing the basil leaves.

4 Heat a little oil in a heavy-based pan. Carefully add the basil leaves—stand well away from the pan and protect your hand with a dish cloth, as they may spit a little. Cook for about 30 seconds, or until they begin to curl up, but not brown. Transfer to paper towels to drain.

5 Transfer the cooked chicken, vegetables, and pan juices to to a warm

serving plate and garnish with the deep-fried crispy basil leaves.

COOK'S TIP

Basil has a very strong flavor which is perfect with chicken and Chinese flavorings. You could use baby spinach instead of the basil, if desired.

Stir-Fried Garlic Chicken with Cilantro & Lime

Serves 4

INGREDIENTS

4 large skinless, boneless
    chicken breasts
4 tbsp garlic butter, softened

3 tbsp chopped fresh cilantro
1 tbsp sunflower oil
finely grated zest and juice of 2 limes

4 tbsp palm or brown sugar
boiled rice, to serve

1 Place each chicken breast between 2 sheets of plastic wrap and pound with a rolling pin until flattened to about ½ inch thick.

2 Mix together the garlic butter and cilantro and spread the mixture over each flattened chicken breast. Roll up like a jelly roll and secure with a toothpick.

3 Heat the oil in a wok. Add the chicken rolls and cook, turning frequently, for 15–20 minutes, or until cooked.

4 Remove the chicken from the wok and transfer to a board. Cut each chicken roll into slices.

5 Add the lime zest, juice, and sugar to the wok and heat gently, stirring, until the sugar has dissolved. Increase the heat and allow to bubble for 2 minutes.

6 Arrange the chicken on warm serving plates and spoon the pan juices over it to serve.

7 Garnish with extra fresh cilantro, if desired.

COOK'S TIP

Be sure to check that the chicken is cooked through before slicing and serving. Cook over a gentle heat to avoid overcooking the outside, while the inside remains raw.

Stir-Fried Chicken with Cumin Seeds & Eggplant

Serves 4

INGREDIENTS

5 tbsp sunflower oil

2 cloves garlic, crushed

1 tbsp cumin seeds

1 tbsp mild curry powder

1 tbsp paprika

1 pound boneless, skinless
chicken breasts

1 large eggplant, cubed

4 tomatoes, cut into quarters

½ cup chicken stock

1 tbsp fresh lemon juice

½ tsp salt

⅔ cup unsweetened yogurt

1 tbsp chopped fresh mint

1 Heat 2 tablespoons of the sunflower oil in a large preheated wok.

2 Add the garlic, cumin seeds, curry powder, and paprika to the wok and stir-fry for 1 minute.

3 Using a sharp knife, thinly slice the chicken breasts.

4 Add the rest of the oil to the wok and stir-fry the chicken for 5 minutes.

5 Add the eggplant cubes, tomatoes, and chicken stock and bring to a boil. Reduce the heat slightly and simmer for about 20 minutes.

6 Stir in the lemon juice, salt, and yogurt and cook over a gentle heat for a further 5 minutes, stirring occasionally.

7 Scatter with chopped fresh mint and transfer to serving bowls. Serve at once.

COOK'S TIP

Once the yogurt has been added, do not boil the sauce as the yogurt will curdle.

Speedy Peanut Pan-Fry

Serves 4

INGREDIENTS

2 cups zucchini	1 tablespoon sesame oil	peanut butter
1⅓ cups baby corn	8 boneless chicken thighs	2 tablespoons soy sauce
3¾ cups button mushrooms	or 4 breasts, thinly sliced	2 tablespoons lime or lemon juice
3 cups thread egg noodles	1½ cups bean sprouts	½ cup roasted peanuts
2 tablespoons corn oil	4 tablespoons smooth	pepper
		cilantro, to garnish

1 Using a sharp knife, trim and thinly slice the zucchini, baby corn, and button mushrooms.

2 Bring a large pan of lightly salted water to a boil and cook the noodles for 3–4 minutes. Meanwhile, heat together the corn oil and sesame oil in a large skillet or wok. Add the chicken and fry over fairly high heat for 1 minute.

3 Add the sliced zucchini, baby corn, and button mushrooms and stir-fry for 5 minutes.

4 Add the bean sprouts, peanut butter, soy sauce, lime or lemon juice, and pepper, then cook for a further 2 minutes.

5 Drain the noodles, transfer to a serving dish, and scatter with the peanuts. Serve with the stir-fried chicken and vegetables, garnished with a sprig of fresh cilantro.

COOK'S TIP

Try serving this stir-fry with rice sticks. These are broad, pale, translucent ribbon noodles made from ground rice.

Hoisin Duck with Leek & Stir-Fried Cabbage

Serves 4

INGREDIENTS

4 duck breasts

12 ounces green cabbage, outer leaves and stems removed

8 ounces leeks, sliced

finely grated zest of 1 orange

6 tbsp oyster sauce

1 tsp toasted sesame seeds, to serve

1 Heat a large wok and dry-fry the duck breasts, with the skin on, for 5 minutes on each side (you may need to do this in 2 batches).

2 Remove the duck breasts from the wok and transfer to a clean board. Using a sharp knife, cut the duck breasts into thin slices.

3 Remove all but 1 tablespoon of the fat from the duck left in the wok; discarding the rest.

4 Using a sharp knife, thinly shred the green cabbage.

5 Add the leeks, green cabbage, and orange zest to the wok and stir-fry for 5 minutes, or until the vegetables have softened.

6 Return the duck to the wok and heat through for 2–3 minutes.

7 Drizzle the oyster sauce over the top of the duck, toss well to combine, and then heat through.

8 Scatter with toasted sesame seeds and serve hot.

VARIATION

Use Chinese cabbage for a lighter, sweeter flavor instead of the green cabbage, if desired.

Duck with Baby Corn Cobs & Pineapple

Serves 4

INGREDIENTS

4 duck breasts	8 ounces baby onions, peeled	6 scallions, sliced
1 tsp Chinese five-spice powder	2 cloves garlic, crushed	1/2 cup bean sprouts
1 tbsp cornstarch	1 cup baby corn cobs	2 tbsp plum sauce
1 tbsp chili oil	1 1/4 cups canned pineapple chunks	

1 Remove any skin from the duck breasts. Cut the duck breasts into thin slices.

2 Mix together the Chinese five-spice powder and the cornstarch in a large bowl.

3 Toss the duck in the five-spice powder and cornstarch mixture until well coated.

4 Heat the oil in a large preheated wok. Stir-fry the duck for about 10 minutes, or until just beginning to go crisp around the edges.

5 Remove the duck from the wok and set aside until it is required.

6 Add the onions and garlic to the wok and stir-fry for 5 minutes, or until the onions have softened.

7 Add the baby corn cobs to the wok and stir-fry for a further 5 minutes.

8 Add the pineapple chunks, scallions, and bean sprouts and stir-fry for 3–4 minutes. Stir in the plum sauce.

9 Return the cooked duck to the wok and toss until well mixed. Transfer to warm serving dishes and serve hot.

COOK'S TIP

Buy pineapple chunks in natural juice rather than syrup for a fresher flavor. If you can obtain only pineapple in syrup, rinse it in cold water and drain thoroughly before using.

Stir-Fried Turkey with Cranberry Glaze

Serves 2–3

INGREDIENTS

1 turkey breast	¹/₂ cup fresh or frozen cranberries	3 tbsp light soy sauce
2 tbsp sunflower oil	¹/₄ cup canned chestnuts	salt and pepper
2 tbsp preserved ginger	4 tbsp cranberry sauce	

1 Remove any skin from the turkey breast. Using a sharp knife, thinly slice the turkey breast.

2 Heat the oil in a large preheated wok.

3 Add the turkey to the wok and stir-fry for 5 minutes, or until cooked through.

4 Using a sharp knife, finely chop the preserved ginger.

5 Add the ginger and the cranberries to the wok and stir-fry for 2–3 minutes, or until the cranberries have softened.

6 Add the chestnuts, cranberry sauce, and soy sauce, season to taste with salt and pepper, and allow to bubble for 2–3 minutes.

7 Transfer to warm serving dishes and serve immediately.

COOK'S TIP

If you wish, use a turkey escalope instead of the breast for really tender, lean meat.

COOK'S TIP

It is very important that the wok is very hot before you stir-fry. This can be tested by holding your hand flat about 3 inches above the base of the interior – you should be able to feel the heat radiating from it.

Stir-Fried Beef & Vegetables with Sherry & Soy Sauce

Serves 4

INGREDIENTS

2 tbsp sunflower oil

12 ounces fillet of beef, sliced

1 red onion, sliced

8 ounces zucchini

5 medium carrots, thinly sliced

1 red bell pepper, seeded and sliced

1 small head Chinese cabbage, shredded

¾ cup bean sprouts

8 ounce can bamboo shoots, drained

¾ cup cashew nuts, toasted

SAUCE:

3 tbsp medium sherry

3 tbsp light soy sauce

1 tsp ground ginger

1 clove garlic, crushed

1 tsp cornstarch

1 tbsp tomato paste

1 Heat the sunflower oil in a large preheated wok.

2 Add the beef and onion to the wok and stir-fry for 4–5 minutes, or until the onion begins to soften and the meat is just browning.

3 Using a sharp knife, trim the zucchini and thinly slice diagonally.

4 Add the carrots, bell pepper, and zucchini, and stir-fry for 5 minutes.

5 Toss in the Chinese cabbage, bean sprouts, and bamboo shoots and heat through for 2–3 minutes, or until the cabbage is just beginning to wilt.

6 Scatter the cashews nuts over the stir-fry.

7 To make the sauce, mix together the sherry, soy sauce, ground ginger, garlic, cornstarch, and tomato paste. to make a smooth paste. Pour the sauce over the stir-fry and toss until well combined. Allow the sauce to bubble for 2–3 minutes, or until the juices start to thicken.

8 Transfer to warm serving dishes and serve at once.

Chili Beef Stir-Fry Salad

Serves 4

INGREDIENTS

1 pound lean steak
2 cloves garlic, crushed
1 tsp chili powder
½ tsp salt
1 tsp ground coriander

1 ripe avocado
2 tbsp sunflower oil
15 ounce can red kidney
   beans, drained
6 ounces cherry tomatoes, halved

1 large packet tortilla chips
shredded iceberg lettuce
chopped fresh cilantro,
   to serve

1 Using a sharp knife, slice the steak into thin strips.

2 Place the garlic, chili powder, salt, and ground coriander in a large bowl and mix until thoroughly combined.

3 Add the strips of steak to the marinade and toss well to coat all over.

4 Using a sharp knife, peel the avocado. Slice the avocado lengthwise and then crosswise to form small dice.

5 Heat the oil in a large preheated wok. Add the steak and stir-fry, tossing frequently, for 5 minutes, until browned.

6 Add the kidney beans, tomatoes, and avocado and heat through for 2 minutes.

7 Arrange a bed of tortilla chips and iceberg lettuce around the edge of a large serving plate and spoon the steak mixture into the center. Alternatively, serve the steak and hand the tortilla chips and iceberg lettuce separately.

8 Garnish with chopped fresh cilantro and serve immediately.

COOK'S TIP

Serve this dish immediately, as avocado tends to discolor quickly. Once you have cut the avocado into dice, sprinkle it with a little lemon juice to prevent discoloration.

Marinated Beef Stir-Fry with Bamboo Shoots & Snow Peas

Serves 4

INGREDIENTS

12 ounces steak	1 tbsp fresh lemon juice	7 ounce can bamboo shoots,
3 tbsp dark soy sauce	1 tsp ground coriander	drained
1 tbsp tomato ketchup	2 tbsp vegetable oil	1 tsp sesame oil
2 cloves garlic, crushed	2³/₄ cups snow peas	

1 Using a sharp knife, thinly slice the steak.

2 Place the meat in a nonmetallic dish, together with the dark soy sauce, tomato ketchup, garlic, lemon juice, and ground coriander. Mix well so that all of the steak is coated in the marinade, cover, and set aside for at least 1 hour.

3 Heat the vegetable oil in a preheated wok. Add the steak to the wok and stir-fry for 2–4 minutes, depending on how well

cooked you like your meat, or until cooked through.

4 Add the snow peas and bamboo shoots to the mixture in the wok and stir-fry over a high heat, tossing frequently, for a further 5 minutes.

5 Drizzle with the sesame oil and toss well to combine.

6 Transfer to serving dishes and serve hot.

COOK'S TIP

Marinate the steak for at least 1 hour in order for the flavor to penetrate and increase the tenderness of the meat. If possible, marinate for a little longer for a fuller flavor to develop.

Stir-Fried Beef with Baby Onions & Palm Sugar

Serves 4

INGREDIENTS

1 pound beef fillet	1 tbsp tamarind paste	2 tbsp sunflower oil
2 tbsp soy sauce	2 tbsp palm or brown sugar	8 ounces baby onions
1 tsp chili oil	2 cloves garlic, crushed	2 tbsp chopped fresh cilantro

1 Using a sharp knife, thinly slice the beef.

2 Place the slices of beef in a single layer in a large, shallow nonmetallic dish.

3 Mix together the soy sauce, chili oil, tamarind paste, sugar, and garlic.

4 Spoon the sugar mixture over the beef. Toss well to coat the beef in the mixture, cover, and set aside in the refrigerator to marinate for at least 1 hour.

5 Heat the sunflower oil in a preheated wok.

6 Peel the onions and cut them in half. Add the onions to the wok and stir-fry for 2–3 minutes, or until just browning.

7 Add the beef and marinade juices to the wok and stir-fry over a high heat for about 5 minutes.

8 Scatter with chopped fresh cilantro, transfer to a warm serving dish, and serve at once.

COOK'S TIP

Use the chili oil carefully as it is very hot and could easily spoil the dish if too much is added.

Sweet Potato Stir-Fry with Coconut Beef

Serves 4

INGREDIENTS

2 tbsp vegetable oil	1 onion, sliced	1¼ cups coconut milk
12 ounces steak	12 ounces sweet potatoes	3 limes leaves
2 cloves garlic	2 tbsp Thai red curry paste	cooked jasmine rice, to serve

1 Heat the vegetable oil in a large preheated wok.

2 Using a sharp knife, thinly slice the steak. Add the steak to the wok and stir-fry for about 2 minutes, or until sealed on all sides.

3 Add the garlic and the onion to the wok and stir-fry for a further 2 minutes.

4 Using a sharp knife, peel and dice the sweet potatoes.

5 Add the sweet potatoes to the wok with the curry paste, coconut milk and lime leaves and bring to a rapid boil. Reduce the heat, cover, and simmer for about 15 minutes, or until the sweet potatoes are tender.

6 Remove the lime leaves and transfer the stir-fry to warm serving bowls. Serve hot with cooked jasmine rice.

COOK'S TIP

There are two basic curry pastes used in Thai cuisine—red and green, depending on whether they are made from red or green chilies.

COOK'S TIP

If you cannot obtain lime leaves, use grated lime zest instead.

Beef with Green Peas & Black Bean Sauce

Serves 4

INGREDIENTS

1 pound steak	2 cloves garlic, crushed	5½ ounces Chinese
2 tbsp sunflower oil	1¼ cup fresh or frozen peas	cabbage, shredded
1 onion	5¾ ounce jar black bean sauce	

1 Using a sharp knife, trim away any fat from the steak. Cut the steak into thin slices.

2 Heat the sunflower oil in a large preheated wok.

3 Add the steak to the wok and stir-fry for 2 minutes.

4 Using a sharp knife, peel and slice the onion.

5 Add the onion, garlic, and peas to the wok and stir-fry for a further 5 minutes.

6 Add the black bean sauce and Chinese cabbage to the mixture in the wok and heat through for a further 2 minutes, or until the cabbage has wilted.

7 Transfer to warm serving bowls and serve immediately.

COOK'S TIP

Chinese cabbage is now widely available. It looks like a pale, elongated head of lettuce with light green, tightly packed crinkly leaves.

COOK'S TIP

Buy a chunky black bean sauce if you can for the best texture and flavor.

Pork Tenderloin Stir-Fry with Crunchy Satay Sauce

Serves 4

INGREDIENTS

2-3 medium carrots
2 tbsp sunflower oil
350g/12 ounces pork tenderloin,
    thinly sliced
1 onion, sliced

2 cloves garlic, crushed
1 yellow bell pepper, seeded
    and sliced
2⅓ cups snow peas
1½ cups fine asparagus
chopped salted peanuts, to serve

SATAY SAUCE:
6 tbsp crunchy peanut butter
6 tbsp coconut milk
1 tsp chili flakes
1 clove garlic, crushed
1 tsp tomato paste

1 Using a sharp knife, slice the carrots into thin sticks.

2 Heat the oil in a large, preheated wok. Add the pork, onion, and garlic and stir-fry for 5 minutes, or until the lamb is cooked through.

3 Add the carrots, bell pepper, snow peas, and asparagus to the wok and stir-fry for 5 minutes.

4 To make the satay sauce, place the peanut butter, coconut milk, chili flakes, garlic, and tomato paste in a small pan and heat gently, stirring, until well combined.

5 Transfer the stir-fry to warm serving plates. Spoon the satay sauce over the stir-fry and scatter with coarsely chopped peanuts. Serve immediately.

COOK'S TIP

Cook the sauce just before serving as it tends to thicken very quickly and will not be spoonable if you cook it too far in advance.

Chinese Five-Spice Crispy Pork with Egg Fried Rice

Serves 4

INGREDIENTS

1¼ cups long grain white rice
2½ cups cold water
12 ounces pork tenderloin
2 tsp Chinese five-spice powder
4 tbsp cornstarch

3 large eggs, beaten
2 tbsp sugar
2 tbsp sunflower oil
1 onion
2 cloves garlic, crushed

1-2 medium carrots, diced
1 red bell pepper, seeded and diced
¾ cup peas
2 tbsp butter
salt and pepper

1 Rinse the rice under cold running water. Place the rice in a large saucepan, add the cold water and a pinch of salt. Bring to a boil, cover, then reduce the heat, and simmer for about 10–15 minutes, or until all of the liquid has been absorbed and the rice is tender.

2 Meanwhile, slice the pork tenderloin into very thin pieces, using a sharp knife. Set aside until required.

3 Beat together the five-spice powder, cornstarch, 1 egg, and the sugar. Toss the pork in the mixture until coated.

4 Heat the oil in a large preheated wok. Add the pork and cook over a high heat until the pork is cooked through and crispy. Remove the pork from the wok with a slotted spoon and set aside.

5 Using a sharp knife, dice the onion.

6 Add the onion, garlic, carrots, bell pepper, and peas to the wok and stir-fry for 5 minutes.

7 Return the pork to the wok, together with the cooked rice, and stir-fry for 5 minutes.

8 Heat the butter in a skillet. Add the remaining beaten eggs and cook until set. Turn out onto a clean board and slice thinly. Toss the strips of egg into the rice mixture and serve.

Spicy Pork Balls

Serves 4

INGREDIENTS

1 pound ground pork
2 shallots, finely chopped
2 cloves garlic, crushed
1 tsp cumin seeds
½ tsp chili powder

½ cup whole-wheat bread crumbs
1 egg, beaten
2 tbsp sunflower oil
14 ounce can chopped tomatoes, flavored with chili

2 tbsp soy sauce
7 ounce can water chestnuts, drained
3 tbsp chopped fresh cilantro

1 Place the ground pork in a large mixing bowl. Add the shallots, garlic, cumin seeds, chili powder, bread crumbs, and beaten egg and mix together well.

2 Take small pieces of the mixture and form into balls between the palms of your hands.

3 Heat the sunflower oil in a large preheated wok. Add the pork balls to the wok and stir-fry, in batches, over a high heat for about 5 minutes, or until sealed on all sides.

4 Add the tomatoes, soy sauce, and water chestnuts and bring to a boil. Return the pork balls to the wok, reduce the heat and simmer for 15 minutes.

5 Scatter with chopped fresh cilantro, transfer to a serving dish and serve hot.

COOK'S TIP

Cilantro is also known as Chinese parsley, but has a much stronger flavor and should be used with care. Parsley is not a viable alternative; use basil if cilantro is not available.

COOK'S TIP

Add a few teaspoons of chili sauce to a tin of chopped tomatoes, if you can't find the flavored variety.

Sweet & Sour Pork

Serves 4

INGREDIENTS

1 pound pork tenderloin	1 red bell pepper, seeded	²⁄₃ cup pineapple juice
2 tbsp sunflower oil	and sliced	1 tbsp cornstarch
8 ounces zucchini	1 cup baby corn cobs	2 tbsp soy sauce
1 red onion, cut into thin wedges	1½ cups button mushrooms,	3 tbsp tomato ketchup
2 cloves garlic, crushed	halved	1 tbsp white wine vinegar
3–4 medium carrots, cut into	1¼ cups fresh pineapple, cubed	1 tbsp clear honey
thin sticks	½ cup bean sprouts	

1 Using a sharp knife, thinly slice the pork tenderloin.

2 Heat the oil in a large preheated wok.

3 Add the pork to the wok and stir-fry for 10 minutes, or until the pork is completely cooked through and beginning to turn crispy at the edges.

4 Meanwhile, cut the zucchini into thin sticks.

5 Add the onion, garlic, carrots, zucchini, bell pepper, baby corn cobs, and mushrooms to the wok and stir-fry for a further 5 minutes.

6 Add the pineapple cubes and bean sprouts to the wok and stir-fry for 2 minutes.

7 Mix together the pineapple juice, cornstarch, soy sauce, ketchup, wine vinegar and honey to make a smooth paste.

8 Pour the sweet and sour mixture into the wok and cook over a high heat, tossing frequently, until the juices thicken. Transfer the sweet and sour pork to serving bowls and serve hot.

COOK'S TIP

If you prefer a crisper coating, toss the pork in a mixture of cornstarch and egg white and deep fry in the wok in step 3.

Twice-Cooked Pork with Bell Peppers

Serves 4

INGREDIENTS

½ ounce Chinese dried mushrooms	1 onion, sliced	and diced
1 pound pork leg steaks	1 red bell pepper, seeded and diced	1 yellow bell pepper, seeded and diced
2 tbsp vegetable oil	1 green bell pepper, seeded	4 tbsp oyster sauce

1 Place the mushrooms in a large bowl. Pour over enough boiling water to cover and let stand for 20 minutes.

2 Using a sharp knife, trim any excess fat from the pork steaks. Cut the pork into thin strips.

3 Bring a large saucepan of water to a boil. Add the pork to the boiling water and cook for 5 minutes.

4 Remove the pork from the pan with a slotted spoon and drain thoroughly.

5 Heat the oil in a large preheated wok. Add the pork to the wok and stir-fry for about 5 minutes.

6 Remove the mushrooms from the water and drain thoroughly. Discard the stalks and roughly chop the mushroom caps.

7 Add the mushrooms, onion, and the bell peppers to the wok and stir-fry for 5 minutes.

8 Stir in the oyster sauce and cook for 2–3 minutes. Transfer to serving bowls and serve immediately.

VARIATION

Use open-cap mushrooms, sliced, instead of Chinese mushrooms, if desired.

Pork with White Radish

Serves 4

INGREDIENTS

4 tbsp vegetable oil	8 ounces white radish	3 tbsp soy sauce
1 pound pork tenderloin	2 cloves garlic, crushed	2 tbsp sweet chili sauce
1 eggplant		

1 Heat 2 tablespoons of the vegetable oil in a large preheated wok.

2 Using a sharp knife, thinly slice the pork.

3 Add the slices of pork to the wok and stir-fry for about 5 minutes.

4 Using a sharp knife, trim and finely dice the eggplant. Peel and thinly slice the white radish.

5 Add the remaining vegetable oil to the wok.

6 Add the diced eggplant to the wok, together with the garlic and stir-fry for 5 minutes.

7 Add the white radish to the wok and stir-fry for about 2 minutes.

8 Stir the soy sauce and sweet chili sauce into the mixture in the wok and continue cooking until heated through.

9 Transfer the pork and white radish mixture to warm serving bowls or a large warm serving dish and serve immediately.

COOK'S TIP

Mooli (white radish) are long white vegetables common in Chinese cooking. They are generally available in most large supermarkets. They are usually grated and have a milder flavour than red radish.

Lamb with Satay Sauce

Serves 4

INGREDIENTS

1 pound lamb loin fillet	½ tsp chili powder	6 tbsp crunchy peanut butter
1 tbsp mild curry paste	½ tsp cumin	1 tsp tomato paste
⅔ cup coconut milk	1 tbsp corn oil	1 tsp fresh lime juice
2 cloves garlic, crushed	1 onion, diced	1⅓ cup cold water

1 Using a sharp knife, thinly slice the lamb. Place the lamb in a large dish.

2 Mix together the curry paste, coconut milk, garlic, chili powder, and cumin in a bowl.

3 Pour the mixture over the lamb, toss well, cover, and marinate for 30 minutes.

4 Meanwhile, make the satay sauce. Heat the oil in a large wok. Add the onion and stir-fry for 5 minutes, then reduce the heat, and cook for 5 minutes.

5 Add the peanut butter, tomato paste, lime juice, and cold water to the wok, stirring well to combine.

6 Thread the lamb onto wooden skewers, reserving the marinade.

7 Broil the lamb skewers under a preheated broiler for 6–8 minutes, turning once.

8 Add the reserved marinade to the wok, bring to a boil, and cook for 5 minutes. Serve the lamb skewers with the satay sauce.

COOK'S TIP

Soak the wooden skewers in cold water for 30 minutes before broiling to prevent the skewers from burning.

Stir-Fried Lamb with Black Bean Sauce & Mixed Bell Peppers

Serves 4

INGREDIENTS

1 pound lamb neck fillet or
    boneless leg of lamb chops
1 egg white, lightly beaten
4 tbsp cornstarch
1 tsp Chinese five-spice powder

3 tbsp sunflower oil
1 red onion
1 red bell pepper, seeded and sliced
1 green bell pepper, seeded
    and sliced

1 yellow or orange bell pepper,
    seeded and sliced
5 tbsp black bean sauce
boiled rice or noodles, to serve

1 Using a sharp knife, slice the lamb into very thin strips.

2 Mix the egg white, cornstarch, and Chinese five-spice powder together in a large bowl. Toss the lamb strips in the mixture until evenly coated.

3 Heat the oil in a large preheated wok. Add the lamb and stir-fry over a high heat for 5 minutes, or until it begins to turn crisp around the edges.

4 Using a sharp knife, slice the red onion. Add the onion and bell pepper slices to the wok and stir-fry for 5-6 minutes, or until the vegetables just begin to soften.

5 Stir the black bean sauce into the mixture in the wok and heat through.

6 Transfer the lamb and sauce to warm serving plates and serve hot with freshly boiled rice or noodles.

COOK'S TIP

Take care when frying the lamb as the cornstarch mixture may cause it to stick to the wok. Move the lamb around the wok constantly during stir-frying.

Scallion Onion & Lamb Stir-Fry with Oyster Sauce

Serves 4

INGREDIENTS

1 pound lamb leg steaks	2 cloves garlic, crushed	6 tbsp oyster sauce
1 tsp ground Szechuan peppercorns	8 scallions, sliced	6 ounces Chinese cabbage
1 tbsp peanut oil	2 tbsp dark soy sauce	shrimp crackers, to serve

1 Using a sharp knife, remove any excess fat from the lamb. Slice the lamb thinly.

2 Sprinkle the ground Szechuan peppercorns over the meat and toss together until well combined.

3 Heat the oil in a preheated wok. Add the lamb and stir-fry for 5 minutes.

4 Mix the garlic, scallions, and soy sauce, add to the wok, and stir-fry for 2 minutes.

5 Add the oyster sauce and Chinese cabbage and stir-fry for a further 2 minutes, or until the leaves have wilted and the juices are bubbling.

6 Transfer the stir-fry to warm serving bowls and serve hot.

COOK'S TIP

Oyster sauce is made from oysters which are cooked in brine and soy sauce. Sold in bottles, it will keep in the refrigerator for months.

COOK'S TIP

Shrimp crackers consist of compressed slivers of shrimp and flour paste. They expand when deep-fried.

Curried Stir-Fried Lamb with Diced Potatoes

Serves 4

INGREDIENTS

1 pound potatoes, diced

1 pound lean lamb, cubed

2 tbsp medium hot curry paste

3 tbsp sunflower oil

1 onion, sliced

1 eggplant, diced

2 cloves garlic, crushed

1 tbsp grated fresh ginger root

2/3 cup lamb or beef stock

2 tbsp chopped fresh cilantro

1 Bring a large saucepan of lightly salted water to a boil. Add the potatoes and cook over a medium heat for 10 minutes. Remove the potatoes from the saucepan with a slotted spoon and drain thoroughly.

2 Meanwhile, place the lamb in a large mixing bowl. Add the curry paste and mix until thoroughly combined.

3 Heat the sunflower oil in a large preheated wok.

4 Lower the heat slightly, add the onion, eggplant, garlic, and ginger to the wok, and stir-fry for about 5 minutes.

5 Add the lamb to the wok and stir-fry for a further 5 minutes.

6 Add the lamb or beef stock and drained cooked potatoes to the wok, bring to a boil, and simmer for 30 minutes, or until the lamb is tender and completely cooked through.

7 Transfer the stir-fry to warm serving dishes and scatter with chopped fresh cilantro.
Serve immediately.

Garlic-Infused Lamb with Soy Sauce

Serves 4

INGREDIENTS

1 pound lamb loin fillet	3 tbsp dry sherry or Chinese rice	1 tsp cornstarch
2 cloves garlic	wine	2 tbsp cold water
2 tbsp peanut oil	3 tbsp dark soy	2 tbsp butter

1 Using a sharp knife, make small slits in the flesh of the lamb.

2 Carefully peel the cloves of garlic and cut them into slices, using a sharp knife.

3 Push the slices of garlic into the slits in the lamb. Place the garlic-infused lamb in a shallow dish.

4 Drizzle 1 tablespoon each of the oil, sherry, and soy sauce over the lamb, cover and set aside to marinate for at least 1 hour, preferably overnight.

5 Using a sharp knife, thinly slice the marinated lamb.

6 Heat the remaining oil in a preheated wok. Add the lamb and stir-fry for 5 minutes.

7 Add the marinade juices and the remaining sherry and soy sauce to the wok and allow the juices to bubble for 5 minutes.

8 Mix the cornstarch with the cold water to make a smooth paste. Add the cornstarch mixture to the wok and cook, stirring occasionally, until the juices start to thicken.

9 Cut the butter into small pieces. Add the butter to the wok and stir until the butter melts. Transfer to serving dishes and serve immediately.

COOK'S TIP

Adding the butter at the end of the recipe gives a glossy, rich sauce which is ideal with the lamb.

Thai-Style Lamb with Lime Leaves

Serves 4

INGREDIENTS

2 red Thai chiles	6 lime leaves	2½ cups coconut milk
2 tbsp peanut oil	1 tbsp tamarind paste	6 ounces cherry tomatoes, halved
2 cloves garlic, crushed	2 tbsp palm or brown sugar	1 tbsp chopped fresh cilantro
4 shallots, chopped	1 pound lean lamb (leg or loin fillet)	fragrant rice, to serve
2 stalks lemon grass, sliced		

1 Using a sharp knife, seed and very finely chop the Thai red chiles.

2 Heat the peanut oil in a large preheated wok.

3 Add the garlic, shallots, lemon grass, lime leaves, tamarind paste, palm or brown sugar, and chiles to the wok and stir-fry for about 2 minutes.

4 Using a sharp knife, cut the lamb into thin strips or cubes.

5 Add the lamb to the wok and stir-fry for about 5 minutes, tossing well so that the lamb is evenly coated in the spice mixture.

6 Pour the coconut milk into the wok and bring to a boil. Reduce the heat and simmer for 20 minutes.

7 Add the cherry tomatoes and chopped fresh cilantro to the wok and simmer for 5 minutes. Transfer to individual warm serving plates and serve hot with fragrant rice.

COOK'S TIP

Thai limes, also known as makut, differ from the common lime in that the leaves are highly scented and the fruits resemble knobby balls. Thai lime leaves are often used in cooking for flavor.

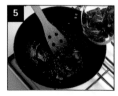

Stir-Fried Lamb with Orange

Serves 4

INGREDIENTS

1 pound ground lamb
2 cloves garlic, crushed
1 tsp cumin seeds
1 tsp ground coriander

1 red onion, sliced
finely grated zest and juice of
 1 orange
2 tbsp soy sauce

1 orange, peeled and segmented
salt and pepper
snipped fresh chives, to garnish

1 Add the ground lamb to a preheated wok. Dry fry the ground lamb for 5 minutes, or until the meat is evenly browned. Drain away any excess fat from the wok.

2 Add the garlic, cumin seeds, coriander, and red onion to the wok and stir-fry for a further 5 minutes.

3 Stir in the finely grated orange zest and juice and the soy sauce, cover, reduce the heat, and simmer, stirring occasionally, for 15 minutes.

4 Remove the lid, raise the heat, add the orange segments, and salt and pepper to taste and heat through for a further 2–3 minutes.

5 Transfer to warm serving plates and garnish with snipped fresh chives. Serve immediately.

VARIATION

Use lime or lemon juice and zest instead of the orange, if wished.

COOK'S TIP

If you wish to serve wine with your meal, try light, dry white wines and lighter Burgundy-style red wines as they blend well with Asian food.

Lamb's Liver with Green Bell Peppers & Sherry

Serves 4

INGREDIENTS

1 pound lamb's liver	2 cloves garlic, crushed	3 tbsp dry sherry
2 tbsp cornstarch	2 green bell peppers, seeded	1 tbsp cornstarch
2 tbsp peanut oil	and sliced	2 tbsp soy sauce
1 onion, sliced	2 tbsp tomato paste	

1 Using a sharp knife, trim any excess fat and the membranes from the lamb's liver. Slice the lamb's liver into thin, even-size strips.

2 Place the cornstarch in a large bowl.

3 Add the strips of lamb's liver to the cornstarch and toss well until coated evenly all over.

4 Heat the peanut oil in a large preheated wok.

5 Add the lamb's liver, onion, garlic, and green bell pepper to the wok and stir-fry for 6–7 minutes, or until the lamb's liver is just cooked through and the vegetables are tender.

6 Mix together the tomato paste, sherry, cornstarch, and soy sauce to make a smooth paste. Stir the mixture into the wok and cook for a further 2 minutes, or until the juices have thickened. Transfer to warm serving bowls and serve immediately.

VARIATION

Use rice wine instead of the sherry for a really authentic Asian flavor. Chinese rice wine is made from glutinous rice and is also known as "yellow wine" because of its golden color. The best variety, from Southeast China, is called Shao Hsing or Shaoxing.

Chilli Chicken

Serves 4

INGREDIENTS

350 g/12 oz skinless, boneless
 lean chicken
1/2 tsp salt
1 egg white, lightly beaten
2 tbsp cornflour (cornstarch)
4 tbsp vegetable oil
2 garlic cloves, crushed

1-cm/1/2-inch piece fresh root
 ginger, grated
1 red (bell) pepper, seeded and
 diced
1 green (bell) pepper, seeded
 and diced
2 fresh red chillies, chopped

2 tbsp light soy sauce
1 tbsp dry sherry or Chinese
 rice wine
1 tbsp wine vinegar

1 Cut the chicken into cubes and place in a mixing bowl. Add the salt, egg white, cornflour (cornstarch) and 1 tbsp of the oil. Turn the chicken in the mixture to coat well.

2 Heat the remaining oil in a preheated wok. Add the garlic and ginger and stir-fry for 30 seconds.

3 Add the chicken pieces to the wok and stir-fry for 2–3 minutes, or until browned.

4 Stir in the (bell) peppers, chillies, soy sauce, sherry or Chinese rice wine and wine vinegar and cook for 2–3 minutes, until the chicken is cooked through. Transfer to a serving dish and serve.

VARIATION

This recipe works well if you use 350 g/12 oz lean steak, cut into thin strips or 450 g/ 1 lb raw prawns (shrimp) instead of the chicken.

COOK'S TIP

When preparing chillies, wear rubber gloves to prevent the juices from burning and irritating your hands. Be careful not to touch your face, especially your lips or eyes, until you have washed your hands.

Lemon Chicken

Serves 4

INGREDIENTS

vegetable oil, for deep-frying	SAUCE:
650 g/1¹/₂ lb skinless, boneless chicken, cut into strips	1 tbsp cornflour (cornstarch)
	6 tbsp cold water
lemon slices and shredded spring onions (scallions), to garnish	3 tbsp fresh lemon juice
	2 tbsp sweet sherry
	¹/₂ tsp caster (superfine) sugar

1 Heat the oil in a wok until almost smoking. Reduce the heat and stir-fry the chicken strips for 3–4 minutes, until cooked through. Remove the chicken with a slotted spoon, set aside and keep warm. Drain the oil from the wok.

2 To make the sauce, mix the cornflour with 2 tablespoons of the water to form a paste.

3 Pour the lemon juice and remaining water into the mixture in the wok. Add the sherry and sugar and bring to the boil, stirring until the sugar has completely dissolved.

4 Stir in the cornflour mixture and return to the boil. Reduce the heat and simmer, stirring constantly, for 2-3 minutes, until the sauce is thickened and clear.

5 Transfer the chicken to a warm serving plate and pour the sauce over the top. Garnish with the lemon slices and shredded spring onions (scallions) and serve immediately.

COOK'S TIP

If you would prefer to use chicken portions rather than strips, cook them in the oil, covered, over a low heat for about 30 minutes, or until cooked through.

Braised Chicken

Serves 4

INGREDIENTS

3 pounds 5 ounces whole chicken	2 tbsp dark brown sugar	1 small onion, chopped
3 tbsp vegetable oil	5 tbsp dark soy sauce	1 fresh red chili, chopped
1 tbsp peanut oil	$^2/_3$ cup water	celery leaves and chives, to garnish
	2 garlic cloves, crushed	

1 Thoroughly clean the chicken inside and out with damp paper towels.

2 Put the oil in a large wok, add the sugar, and heat gently until the sugar caramelizes. Stir in the soy sauce. Add the chicken and turn it in the mixture to coat thoroughly on all sides.

3 Add the water, garlic, onion, and chili. Cover and simmer, turning the chicken occasionally, for about 1 hour, or until cooked through. Test by piercing a thigh with the point of a sharp knife—the juices will run clear when the chicken is cooked.

4 Remove the chicken from the wok and set aside. Increase the heat and reduce the sauce in the wok until thickened. Cut chicken into portions, garnish with celery leaves and chives, and serve with the sauce.

COOK'S TIP

When caramelizing the sugar, do not turn the heat too high, otherwise it may burn.

VARIATION

For a spicier sauce, add 1 tbsp finely chopped fresh ginger root and 1 tbsp ground Szechuan peppercorns with the chili in step 3. If the flavor of dark soy sauce is too strong for your taste, substitute 2 tbsp dark soy sauce and 3 tbsp light soy sauce. This will result in a more delicate taste without sacrificing the attractive color of the dish.

Chicken Chop Suey

Serves 4

INGREDIENTS

4 tbsp light soy sauce
2 tsp light brown sugar
1¼ pounds skinless, boneless
    chicken breasts

3 tbsp vegetable oil
2 onions, quartered
2 garlic cloves, crushed
12 ounces bean sprouts

1 tbsp sesame oil
1 tbsp cornstarch
3 tbsp water
2 cups chicken stock
shredded leek, to garnish

1 Mix the soy sauce and sugar together, stirring until the sugar has dissolved.

2 Trim any fat from the chicken and cut the meat into thin strips. Place the chicken strips in a shallow glass dish and spoon the soy mixture over them, turning to coat. Marinate in the refrigerator for 20 minutes.

3 Heat the oil in a preheated wok. Add the chicken and stir-fry for 2–3 minutes, until golden brown.

4 Add the onions and garlic and cook for a further 2 minutes. Add the bean sprouts, cook for a further 4–5 minutes, then add the sesame oil.

5 Blend the cornstarch with the water to form a smooth paste. Pour the chicken stock into the wok, together with the cornstarch paste, and bring the mixture to a boil, stirring constantly until the sauce is thickened and clear. Transfer to a warm serving dish, garnish with shredded leek, and serve immediately.

VARIATION

This recipe may be made with strips of lean steak, pork, or with mixed vegetables. Change the type of stock accordingly.

Chicken with Yellow Bean Sauce

Serves 4

INGREDIENTS

1 pound skinless, boneless chicken breasts	1 tbsp light soy sauce	1 green bell pepper, seeded and diced
1 egg white, beaten	1 tsp superfine sugar	2 large mushrooms, sliced
1 tbsp cornstarch	3 tbsp vegetable oil	3 tbsp yellow bean sauce
1 tbsp rice wine vinegar	1 garlic clove, crushed	yellow or green bell pepper strips, to garnish
	$\frac{1}{2}$-inch piece fresh ginger root, grated	

1 Trim any fat from the chicken and cut the meat into 1-inch cubes.

2 Mix the egg white and cornstarch in a shallow bowl. Add the chicken and turn in the mixture to coat. Set aside for 20 minutes.

3 Mix the vinegar, soy sauce, and sugar in a bowl.

4 Remove the chicken from the egg white mixture.

5 Heat the oil in a preheated wok, add the chicken, and stir-fry for 3–4 minutes, until golden brown. Remove the chicken from the wok with a slotted spoon, set aside, and keep warm.

6 Stir-fry the garlic, ginger, bell pepper, and mushrooms for 1–2 minutes.

7 Add the yellow bean sauce and cook for 1 minute. Stir in the vinegar mixture and return the chicken to the wok. Cook

for 1–2 minutes and serve hot, garnished with bell pepper strips.

VARIATION

Black bean sauce would work equally well with this recipe. Although this would affect the appearance of the dish, as it is much darker in color, the flavors would be compatible.

Crispy Chicken

Serves 4

INGREDIENTS

3 pounds 5 ounces whole
    chicken
2 tbsp clear honey

2 tsp Chinese five-spice powder
2 tbsp rice wine vinegar

3³/₄ cups vegetable oil, for frying
chili sauce, to serve

1 Rinse the chicken inside and out under cold running water and pat dry with paper towels.

2 Bring a large saucepan of water to a boil and remove from the heat. Place the chicken in the water, cover, and set aside for 20 minutes. Remove the chicken from the water and pat dry with paper towels. Cool and chill in the refrigerator for 8 hours or overnight.

3 To make the glaze, mix together the clear honey, Chinese five-spice powder, and rice wine vinegar.

4 Brush some of the glaze all over the chicken and return to the refrigerator for 20 minutes. Repeat this process until all the glaze has been used up. Return the chicken to the refrigerator for at least 2 hours after the final coating.

5 Using a cleaver or heavy kitchen knife, open the chicken out by splitting it through the center through the breast, and then cut each half into 4 pieces.

6 Heat the oil for deep-frying in a wok until almost smoking. Reduce the heat and fry each piece

of chicken for 5–7 minutes, until golden and cooked through. Remove from the oil with a slotted spoon and drain on absorbent paper towels.

7 Transfer to a warm serving dish and serve hot with a little chili sauce.

COOK'S TIP

If it is easier, use chicken portions instead of a whole chicken. You could also use chicken legs for this recipe, if desired.

Spicy Peanut Chicken

Serves 4

INGREDIENTS

10¹/₂ ounces skinless, boneless
    chicken breast
2 tbsp peanut oil
1 cup unsalted peanuts
1 fresh red chili, sliced
1 green bell pepper, seeded and
    cut into strips

1 tsp sesame oil
fried rice, to serve

SAUCE:
²/₃ cup chicken stock
1 tbsp Chinese rice wine or
    dry sherry

1 tbsp light soy sauce
1¹/₂ tsp light brown sugar
2 garlic cloves, crushed
1 tsp grated fresh ginger root
1 tsp rice wine vinegar

1 Trim any fat from the chicken and cut the meat into 1-inch cubes. Set aside.

2 Heat the peanut oil in a preheated wok. Add the peanuts and stir-fry for 1 minute. Remove the peanuts with a slotted spoon and set aside.

3 Add the chicken to the wok and cook for 1–2 minutes. Stir in the chili and green bell pepper and cook for 1 minute. Remove from the wok with a slotted spoon and set aside.

4 Put half the peanuts in a food processor and process until almost smooth. Alternatively, place them in a plastic bag and crush them with a rolling pin.

5 To make the sauce, add the chicken stock, Chinese rice wine or dry sherry, soy sauce, sugar, garlic, ginger, and rice wine vinegar to the wok.

6 Heat the sauce gently and stir in the peanut purée, peanuts, chicken, chili, and bell pepper.

7 Sprinkle the sesame oil into the wok, stir, and cook for 1 minute. Serve hot with fried rice.

COOK'S TIP

If necessary, process the peanuts with a little of the stock in step 4 to form a softer paste.

Chinese Chicken Salad

Serves 4

INGREDIENTS

8 ounces skinless, boneless
chicken breasts
2 tsp light soy sauce
1 tsp sesame oil
1 tsp sesame seeds
2 tbsp vegetable oil
4¹/₂ ounces bean sprouts

1 red bell pepper, seeded and
thinly sliced
1 carrot, peeled and cut into
matchsticks
3 baby corncobs, sliced
chives and carrot matchsticks, to
garnish

SAUCE:
2 tsp rice wine vinegar
1 tbsp light soy sauce
dash of chili oil

1 Place the chicken in a
shallow glass dish.

2 Mix together the soy
sauce and sesame oil
and pour the mixture over
the chicken. Sprinkle with
sesame seeds and let stand
for 20 minutes.

3 Remove the chicken
from the marinade and
cut the meat into slices.

4 Heat the oil in a
preheated wok. Add
the chicken and fry for 4-5

minutes, until cooked
through and golden brown
on both sides. Remove the
chicken from the wok, and
let cool.

5 Add the bean sprouts,
bell pepper, carrot,
and baby corncobs to the
wok and stir-fry for 2–3
minutes. Remove from the
wok and cool.

6 To make the sauce, mix
the rice wine vinegar,
light soy sauce, and chili
oil together.

7 Arrange the chicken
and vegetables on a
serving plate. Spoon the
sauce over the salad, garnish
with snipped chives and
carrot matchsticks, and serve.

COOK'S TIP

*If you have time, make the
sauce and let stand for 30
minutes for the flavors to
fully develop.*

Peking Duck

Serves 4

INGREDIENTS

4 pounds duck

7½ cups boiling water

4 tbsp clear honey

2 tsp dark soy sauce

2 tbsp sesame oil

½ cup hoisin sauce

⅔ cup superfine sugar

½ cup water

carrot strips, to garnish

Chinese pancakes, cucumber
   matchsticks, and scallions,
   to serve

1 Place the duck on a rack set over a roasting pan and pour 5 cups of the boiling water over it. Remove the duck and rack and discard the water. Pat dry with paper towels, replace the duck and the rack, and set aside for several hours.

2 Mix together the honey, remaining boiling water, and soy sauce. Brush the mixture over the skin and inside the duck. Reserve the remaining glaze. Set the duck aside for 1 hour, until the glaze has dried.

3 Coat the duck with another layer of glaze. Let dry and repeat until all the glaze is used.

4 Heat the oil and add the hoisin sauce, sugar, and water. Simmer for 2–3 minutes, until thickened. Cool and refrigerate.

5 Cook the duck in a preheated oven at 375°F for 30 minutes. Turn the duck over and cook for 20 minutes. Turn the duck again and cook for 20–30 minutes, or until cooked through and the skin is crisp.

6 Remove the duck from the oven and set aside for 10 minutes. Meanwhile, heat the pancakes in a steamer for 5–7 minutes. Cut the duck into strips, garnish with the carrot strips, and serve with the pancakes, sauce, cucumber matchsticks, and scallions.

Duck in Spicy Sauce

Serves 4

INGREDIENTS

1 tbsp vegetable oil

1 tsp grated fresh ginger root

1 garlic clove, crushed

1 fresh red chili, chopped

12 ounces skinless, boneless
   duck, cut into strips

4½ ounces cauliflower, cut
   into florets

2 ounces snow peas

2 ounces baby corncobs,
   halved lengthwise

1¼ cups chicken stock

1 tsp Chinese five-spice powder

2 tsp Chinese rice wine or dry
   sherry

1 tsp cornstarch

2 tsp water

1 tsp sesame oil

1 Heat the vegetable oil in a preheated wok. Lower the heat slightly and add the ginger, garlic, chili, and duck and stir-fry for 2-3 minutes. Remove from the wok with a slotted spoon and set aside.

2 Add the cauliflower florets, snow peas, and baby corncobs to the wok and stir-fry for 2-3 minutes. Pour off any excess oil from the wok and push the vegetables to one side.

3 Return the duck to the wok and pour in the stock. Sprinkle the Chinese five-spice powder over the top, stir in the rice wine or sherry, and cook over a low heat for about 15 minutes, until the duck is tender.

4 Blend the cornstarch with the water to form a smooth paste and stir into the wok, together with the sesame oil. Bring to a boil, stirring until the sauce has thickened and cleared.

5 Transfer the duck and spicy sauce to a warm serving dish and serve immediately.

COOK'S TIP

Omit the chili for a milder dish, or seed the chili before adding it to remove some of the heat.

Honey-Glazed Duck

Serves 4

INGREDIENTS

1 tsp dark soy sauce
2 tbsp clear honey
1 tsp garlic vinegar

2 garlic cloves, crushed
1 tsp ground star anise
2 tsp cornstarch
2 tsp water

2 large boneless duck breasts,
about 8 ounces each
celery leaves, cucumber matchsticks,
and snipped chives, to garnish

1 Mix together the soy sauce, clear honey, garlic vinegar, garlic, and star anise. Blend the cornstarch with the water to form a smooth paste and stir it into the mixture.

2 Place the duck breasts in a shallow ovenproof dish. Brush with the soy marinade, turning to coat them completely. Cover and marinate in the refrigerator for at least 2 hours, or overnight if possible.

3 Remove the duck from the marinade and cook

in a preheated oven at 425°F for 20–25 minutes, basting frequently with the glaze.

4 Remove the duck from the oven and transfer to a preheated broiler. Broil for about 3–4 minutes to caramelize the top of the duck.

5 Remove the duck from the broiler pan and cut into thin slices. Arrange the duck slices in a warm serving dish, garnish with celery leaves, cucumber matchsticks, and snipped chives, and serve immediately.

COOK'S TIP

If the duck begins to burn slightly while it is cooking in the oven, cover with foil. To be sure the duck breasts are cooked through, insert the point of a sharp knife into the thickest part of the flesh. The juices should run clear.

Duck with Mangoes

Serves 4

INGREDIENTS

2 medium-size ripe mangoes
1¼ cups chicken stock
2 large skinless duck breasts,
    about 8 ounces each
2 garlic cloves, crushed

1 tsp grated fresh ginger root
3 tbsp vegetable oil
1 tsp wine vinegar

1 tsp light soy sauce
1 leek, sliced
chopped fresh parsley, to garnish

1 Peel the mangoes and cut the flesh from each side of the pits. Cut the flesh into strips.

2 Put half the mango pieces and the stock in a food processor and process until smooth. Alternatively, press half the mangoes through a fine strainer and mix with the stock.

3 Rub the garlic and ginger over the duck. Heat the oil in a preheated wok and cook the duck breasts, turning, until sealed. Reserve the oil in

the wok and remove the duck. Place the duck on a rack set over a roasting pan and cook in a preheated oven, at 425°F for 20 minutes, until completely cooked through.

4 Meanwhile, place the mango and stock mixture in a saucepan and add the vinegar and soy sauce. Bring to a boil and cook over a high heat, stirring, until reduced by half.

5 Heat the oil reserved in the wok. Add the leek and remaining mango and

stir-fry for 1 minute. Remove from the wok, transfer to a warm serving dish, and keep warm.

6 Slice the cooked duck breasts and arrange the slices on top of the leek and mango mixture. Pour the sauce over the duck slices, garnish, and serve.

COOK'S TIP

Do not overcook the mango slices in the wok, or stir too vigorously, otherwise they will break up.

Stir-Fried Duck with Broccoli & Bell Peppers

Serves 4

INGREDIENTS

1 egg white	1 yellow bell pepper, seeded	2 tsp Chinese rice wine or dry
2 tbsp cornstarch	and diced	sherry
1 pound skinless, boneless duck	4 1/2 ounces small broccoli florets	1 tsp light brown sugar
vegetable oil, for deep-frying	1 garlic clove, crushed	1/2 cup chicken stock
1 red bell pepper, seeded and diced	2 tbsp light soy sauce	2 tsp sesame seeds

1 Beat the egg white and cornstarch together in a mixing bowl.

2 Cut the duck into 1-inch cubes and stir into the egg white mixture. Let stand for 30 minutes.

3 Heat the oil for deep-frying in a preheated wok until almost smoking. Remove the duck from the egg white mixture, add to the wok, and fry in the oil for 4–5 minutes, until crisp. Remove the duck from the oil with a slotted spoon and drain well on paper towels.

4 Add the bell peppers and broccoli to the wok and stir-fry for 2–3 minutes. Remove with a slotted spoon and drain well on paper towels.

5 Pour all but 2 tablespoons of the oil from the wok and return to the heat. Add the garlic and stir-fry for 30 seconds. Stir in the soy sauce, Chinese rice wine or sherry, sugar, and stock and bring to a boil.

6 Stir in the duck and reserved vegetables and cook for 1–2 minutes.

7 Carefully spoon the duck and vegetables onto a warm serving dish and sprinkle with the sesame seeds. Serve immediately.

Pork with Plums

Serves 4

INGREDIENTS

1 pound pork tenderloin	pinch of ground cinnamon	1 tbsp hoisin sauce
1 tbsp cornstarch	5 tsp vegetable oil	²/₃ cup water
2 tbsp light soy sauce	2 garlic cloves, crushed	dash of chili sauce
2 tbsp Chinese rice wine	2 scallions, chopped	fried plum quarters and scallions,
4 tsp light brown sugar	4 tbsp plum sauce	to garnish

1 Cut the pork tenderloin into thin slices.

2 Mix together the cornstarch, soy sauce, Chinese rice wine, sugar, and ground cinnamon.

3 Place the pork in a shallow dish and pour the cornstarch mixture over it. Cover and marinate for at least 30 minutes.

4 Carefully remove the pork from the dish, reserving the marinade.

5 Heat the oil in a preheated wok. Add the pork and stir-fry for 3–4 minutes, until lightly colored golden brown.

6 Stir in the garlic, scallions, plum sauce, hoisin sauce, water, and chili sauce. Bring the sauce to a boil. Reduce the heat, cover, and simmer for 8–10 minutes, or until the pork is cooked through and tender.

7 Stir in the reserved marinade and cook, stirring, for about 5 minutes.

Transfer to a warm serving dish and garnish with fried plum quarters and scallions. Serve immediately.

VARIATION

Strips of boneless duck meat may be used instead of the pork, if desired.

Deep-Fried Pork Fritters

Serves 4

INGREDIENTS

1 pound pork tenderloin
2 tbsp peanut oil
1¾ cups all-purpose flour
2 tsp baking powder
1 egg, beaten
1 cup milk

pinch of chili powder
vegetable oil, for deep-frying

SAUCE:
2 tbsp dark soy sauce
3 tbsp clear honey

1 tbsp wine vinegar
1 tbsp chopped chives
1 tbsp tomato paste
chives, to garnish

1 Cut the pork tenderloin into 1-inch cubes.

2 Heat the peanut oil in a preheated wok. Add the pork and stir-fry for 2-3 minutes, until sealed. Remove the pork with a slotted spoon and set aside until it is required.

3 Sift the flour and baking powder into a bowl and make a well in the center. Gradually beat in the egg, milk, and chili powder to make a thick batter.

4 Heat the oil for deep-frying until almost smoking, then reduce the heat.

5 Toss the pork pieces in the batter. Add the pork to the wok and deep-fry for 2–3 minutes or until golden brown and cooked through. Remove with a slotted spoon and drain on absorbent paper towels.

6 Mix together the soy sauce, honey, wine vinegar, chives, and tomato paste and spoon into a small serving bowl.

7 Transfer the pork fritters to serving dishes, garnish with chives, and serve with the sauce.

COOK'S TIP

Be careful when heating the oil for deep-frying. It must be heated so that it is almost smoking, then the heat must be reduced immediately. Place the pork in the oil carefully.

Beef & Broccoli Stir-Fry

Serves 4

INGREDIENTS

8 ounces lean steak, trimmed	1/2 tsp Chinese five-spice powder	2/3 cup beef stock
2 garlic cloves, crushed	2 tbsp dark soy sauce	2 tsp cornstarch
dash of chili oil	2 tbsp vegetable oil	4 tsp water
1/2-inch piece fresh ginger root, grated	5 ounces broccoli florets	carrot strips, to garnish
	1 tbsp light soy sauce	

1 Cut the steak into thin strips and place in a shallow glass dish. Mix together the garlic, chili oil, grated ginger, Chinese five-spice powder, and soy sauce in a small bowl and pour the mixture over the beef, tossing to coat the strips evenly. Marinate in the refrigerator for 30 minutes.

2 Heat 1 tablespoon of the oil in a preheated wok. Add the broccoli and stir-fry over a medium heat for 4–5 minutes. Remove from the wok with a slotted spoon and set aside.

3 Heat the remaining vegetable oil in the wok. Add the steak strips, together with the marinade, and stir-fry for about 2-3 minutes, until the steak is browned all over and sealed.

4 Return the broccoli to the wok and stir in the soy sauce and stock.

5 Blend the cornstarch with the water to form a smooth paste and stir it into the wok. Bring to a boil, stirring until thickened and clear. Cook for 1 minute.

6 Transfer the beef and broccoli stir-fry to a warm serving dish, arrange the carrot strips in a lattice pattern on top, and serve immediately.

COOK'S TIP

Marinate the steak for several hours for a fuller flavor. Cover and marinate in the refrigerator if preparing in advance.

Marinated Beef With Oyster Sauce

Serves 4

INGREDIENTS

8 ounces lean steak, cut into
  1-inch cubes
1 tbsp light soy sauce
1 tsp sesame oil
2 tsp Chinese rice wine or
  dry sherry
1 tsp superfine sugar
2 tsp hoisin sauce
1 garlic clove, crushed
$\frac{1}{2}$ tsp cornstarch

2 tbsp vegetable oil
3 garlic cloves, crushed
$\frac{1}{2}$-inch piece fresh ginger
  root, grated
8 baby corncobs, halved
  lengthwise
$\frac{1}{2}$ green bell pepper, seeded and
  thinly sliced
1 ounce canned bamboo shoots,
  drained and rinsed

green bell pepper slices,
  to garnish
rice or noodles, to serve

SAUCE:
2 tbsp dark soy sauce
1 tsp superfine sugar
$\frac{1}{2}$ tsp cornstarch
3 tbsp oyster sauce
8 tbsp water

1 Place the steak in a shallow dish. Mix together the soy sauce, sesame oil, Chinese rice wine or sherry, sugar, hoisin sauce, garlic, and cornstarch and pour the mixture over the steak, turning it to coat. Cover and marinate for at least 1 hour.

2 Meanwhile, make the sauce. Mix the dark soy sauce with the sugar, cornstarch, oyster sauce, and water. Heat the oil in a preheated wok. Add the steak, together with the marinade, and stir-fry for 2–3 minutes, until sealed and lightly browned.

3 Add the garlic, ginger, baby corn cobs, bell pepper, and bamboo shoots. Stir in the oyster sauce mixture and bring to a boil. Reduce the heat and cook for 2–3 minutes. Transfer to a warm serving dish, garnish with green bell pepper slices, and serve immediately with rice or noodles.

COOK'S TIP

For a fuller flavor, marinate the beef in the refrigerator overnight.

Spicy Beef

Serves 4

INGREDIENTS

8 ounces fillet steak	SAUCE:	1 tbsp dry sherry
2 garlic cloves, crushed	2 tbsp vegetable oil	1/4 tsp chili sauce
1 tsp powdered star anise	1 bunch scallions, halved	2/3 cup water
1 tbsp dark soy sauce	lengthwise	2 tsp cornstarch
scallion tassels, to garnish	1 tbsp dark soy sauce	4 tsp water
(optional)		

1 Cut the steak into thin strips and place in a shallow dish.

2 Mix together the garlic, star anise, and dark soy sauce in a bowl and pour the mixture over the steak strips, turning them to ensure that they are thoroughly coated. Cover with plastic wrap and marinate in the refrigerator for at least 1 hour, preferably overnight.

3 Heat the oil in a preheated wok. Reduce the heat slightly, add the halved scallions and stir-fry for 1-2 minutes. Remove from the wok with a slotted spoon and set aside.

4 Add the beef to the wok, together with the marinade, and stir-fry for 3-4 minutes. Return the halved scallions to the wok and add the soy sauce, sherry, chili sauce and the water.

5 Blend the cornstarch to a paste with the 4 tsp water and stir into the wok. Bring to a boil, stirring until the sauce thickens and clears.

6 Transfer to a warm serving dish, garnish with scallion tassels, if using, and serve immediately.

COOK'S TIP

Omit the chili sauce for a milder dish.

Beef & Beans

Serves 4

INGREDIENTS

1 pound fillet steak, cut into
   1-inch pieces

MARINADE:
2 tsp cornstarch
2 tbsp dark soy sauce
2 tsp peanut oil

SAUCE:
2 tbsp vegetable oil
3 garlic cloves, crushed
1 small onion, cut into 8 sections
8 ounces thin green beans,
   halved
1/4 cup unsalted cashews

1 ounce canned bamboo shoots,
   drained and rinsed
2 tsp dark soy sauce
2 tsp Chinese rice wine or dry
   sherry
1/2 cup beef stock
2 tsp cornstarch
4 tsp water
salt and pepper

1 To make the marinade, mix together the cornstarch, soy sauce and peanut oil.

2 Place the steak in a shallow glass bowl. Pour the marinade over the steak, turn to coat thoroughly, cover, and marinate in the refrigerator for at least 30 minutes.

3 To make the sauce, heat the oil in a preheated wok. Lower the heat slightly, add the garlic, onion, beans, cashews, and bamboo shoots, and stir-fry for 2–3 minutes.

4 Remove the steak from the marinade, drain, add to the wok, and stir-fry for 3–4 minutes.

5 Mix the soy sauce, Chinese rice wine or sherry, and beef stock together. Blend the cornstarch with the water to make a smooth paste and add to the soy sauce mixture, mixing to combine.

6 Stir the mixture into the wok and bring the sauce to a boil, stirring until thickened and clear. Reduce the heat and simmer for 2–3 minutes. Season to taste and serve immediately.

Lamb Meatballs

Serves 4

INGREDIENTS

1 pound ground lamb	1 tbsp chopped fresh parsley	1 leek, sliced
3 garlic cloves, crushed	$\frac{1}{2}$ cup fresh white breadcrumbs	1 tbsp cornstarch
2 scallions, finely chopped	1 egg, beaten	2 tbsp water
$\frac{1}{2}$ tsp chili powder	3 tbsp vegetable oil	1$\frac{1}{4}$ cups lamb stock
1 tsp Chinese curry powder	4$\frac{1}{2}$ ounces Chinese	1 tbsp dark soy sauce
	cabbage, shredded	shredded leek, to garnish

1 Mix the lamb, garlic, scallions, chili powder, Chinese curry powder, parsley, and breadcrumbs together in a bowl. Work the egg into the mixture, bringing it together to form a firm mixture. Roll into 16 small, even-size balls.

2 Heat the oil in a preheated wok. Add the cabbage and leek and stir-fry for 1 minute. Remove from the wok with a slotted spoon and set aside.

3 Add the meatballs to the wok and fry in batches, turning gently, for 3-4 minutes, until golden brown all over.

4 Mix the cornstarch and water together to form a smooth paste and set aside. Pour the lamb stock and soy sauce into the wok and cook for 2–3 minutes. Stir in the cornstarch paste. Bring to a boil and cook, stirring constantly, until the sauce has thickened and become clear.

5 Return the cabbage and leek to the wok and cook for 1 minute, until heated through. Arrange the cabbage and leek on a warm serving dish, top with the meatballs, garnish with shredded leek, and serve immediately.

VARIATION

Use ground pork or beef instead of the lamb as an alternative.

226

Lamb with Mushroom Sauce

Serves 4

INGREDIENTS

12 ounces lean boneless lamb, such as fillet or loin	1 tsp cornstarch	$\frac{1}{2}$ tsp chili sauce
2 tbsp vegetable oil	4 tbsp light soy sauce	6 ounces large mushrooms, sliced
3 garlic cloves, crushed	3 tbsp Chinese rice wine or dry sherry	$\frac{1}{2}$ tsp sesame oil
1 leek, sliced	3 tbsp water	fresh red chili strips, to garnish

1 Using a sharp knife, cut the lamb into thin strips.

2 Heat the oil in a preheated wok. Add the lamb strips, garlic, and leek and stir-fry for about 2–3 minutes.

3 Mix together the cornstarch, soy sauce, Chinese rice wine or dry sherry, water, and chili sauce in a bowl until thoroughly combined and set aside.

4 Add the mushrooms to the wok and stir-fry for 1 minute.

5 Stir in the sauce and cook for 2–3 minutes, or until the lamb is cooked through and tender. Sprinkle the sesame oil over the top and transfer to a warm serving dish. Garnish with red chili strips and serve immediately.

COOK'S TIP

Use rehydrated dried Chinese mushrooms obtainable from specialty shops or Chinese grocery stores for a really authentic flavor.

VARIATION

The lamb can be replaced with lean steak or pork tenderloin in this classic recipe from Beijing. You could also use 2–3 scallions, 1 shallot, or 1 small onion instead of the leek, if desired.

Lamb with Garlic Sauce

Serves 4

INGREDIENTS

1 pound lamb fillet or loin

2 tbsp dark soy sauce

2 tsp sesame oil

2 tbsp Chinese rice wine or dry
    sherry

¹/₂ tsp Szechuan pepper

4 tbsp vegetable oil

4 garlic cloves, crushed

2 ounces canned water chestnuts,
    drained and quartered

1 green bell pepper, seeded
    and sliced

1 tbsp wine vinegar

1 tbsp sesame oil

1 Cut the lamb into 1-inch pieces and place them in a shallow dish.

2 Mix together 1 tablespoon of the soy sauce, the sesame oil, Chinese rice wine or sherry, and Szechuan pepper. Pour the mixture over the lamb, turning to coat, and marinate for at least 30 minutes.

3 Heat the vegetable oil in a preheated wok. Remove the lamb from the marinade and add to the wok, together with the garlic. Stir-fry for 2–3 minutes, then remove the lamb from the wok with a slotted spoon, set aside, and keep warm.

4 Add the water chestnuts and bell pepper to the wok and stir-fry for 1 minute. Add the remaining soy sauce and the wine vinegar, mixing well.

5 Return the lamb to the wok and add the sesame oil. Cook, stirring constantly, for 1–2 minutes, or until the lamb is heated through. Transfer to a warm serving dish and serve immediately.

COOK'S TIP

Sesame oil is used as a flavoring, rather than for frying, as it burns readily, hence it is added at the end of cooking.

VARIATION

Chinese chives, also known as garlic chives, would make an appropriate garnish for this dish.

Hot Lamb

Serves 4

INGREDIENTS

1 pound lean, boneless lamb
2 tbsp hoisin sauce
1 tbsp dark soy sauce
1 garlic clove, crushed
2 tsp grated fresh ginger root
2 tbsp vegetable oil
2 onions, sliced

1 fennel bulb, sliced
4 tbsp water

SAUCE:
1 large fresh red chili, cut into
    thin strips

1 fresh green chili, cut into
    thin strips
2 tbsp rice wine vinegar
2 tsp light brown sugar
2 tbsp peanut oil
1 tsp sesame oil

1 Cut the lamb into 1-inch cubes and place in a shallow glass dish.

2 Mix together the hoisin sauce, soy sauce, garlic, and ginger in a bowl and pour over the lamb, turning to coat well. Marinate in the refrigerator for 20 minutes.

3 Heat the vegetable oil in a preheated wok. Add the lamb and stir-fry for 1–2 minutes.

4 Add the onions and fennel to the wok and cook for a further 2 minutes, or until they are just beginning to brown.

5 Stir in the water, cover, and cook for 2–3 minutes.

6 To make the sauce, place the chiles, rice wine vinegar, sugar, peanut oil, and sesame oil in a saucepan and cook over a low heat for 3-4 minutes, stirring to combine.

7 Transfer the lamb and onions to a warm serving dish, pour the sauce on top, toss lightly, and serve immediately.

VARIATION

Use beef, pork, or duck instead of the lamb and vary the vegetables, using leeks or celery instead of the onion and fennel.

Sesame Lamb Stir-Fry

Serves 4

INGREDIENTS

1 pound boneless lean lamb	2 leeks, sliced	1 tbsp dark soy sauce
2 tbsp peanut oil	2 garlic cloves, crushed	4 $\frac{1}{2}$ tsp sesame seeds
1 carrot, peeled and cut into matchsticks	$\frac{1}{3}$ cup lamb or vegetable stock	
	2 tsp light brown sugar	

1 Cut the lamb into thin strips. Heat the peanut oil in a preheated wok. Add the lamb and stir-fry for 2–3 minutes. Remove the lamb from the wok with a slotted spoon and set aside.

2 Add the carrot, leek, and garlic to the wok and stir-fry in the remaining oil for 1–2 minutes. Remove from the wok with a slotted spoon and set aside. Drain any remaining oil.

3 Place the stock, sugar, and soy sauce in the wok and add the lamb.

Cook, stirring constantly to coat the lamb, for 2–3 minutes. Sprinkle the sesame seeds over the top, turning the lamb to coat.

4 Spoon the leek mixture onto a warm serving dish and top with the lamb. Serve immediately.

COOK'S TIP

Be careful not to burn the sugar in the wok when heating and coating the meat, otherwise the flavor of the dish will be spoiled.

VARIATION

This recipe would be equally delicious made with strips of skinless chicken or turkey breast or with shrimp. The cooking times remain the same.

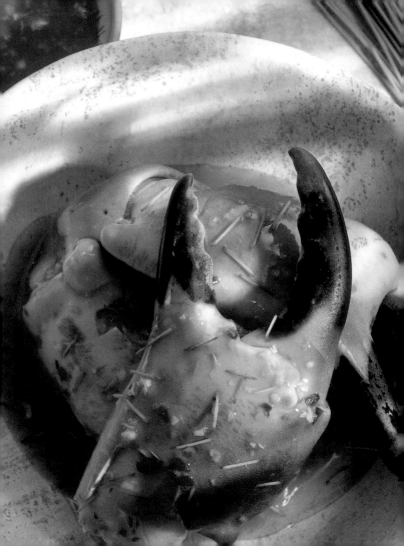

Fish
Seafood

Throughout the Far Eastern countries, fish and seafood play a major role in the diet, as they are both plentiful and healthy. There are many different ways of cooking fish and seafood in a wok – they may be steamed, deep-fried or stir-fried with a range of delicious spices and sauces.

Japan is famed for its sashimi or raw fish, but this is just one of the wide range of fish dishes served. Fish and seafood are offered at every meal in Japan, many of them cooked in a wok. Many unusual and tasty dishes are offered in this chapter, combining fish and seafood with aromatic herbs and spices, pastes and sauces.

When buying fish and seafood for the recipes in this chapter, freshness is imperative to flavour, so be sure to buy and use it as soon as possible, preferably on the same day.

Teriyaki Stir-Fried Salmon with Crispy Leeks

Serves 4

INGREDIENTS

1 pound salmon fillet, skinned	1 tbsp sugar	1 leek, thinly shredded
2 tbsp sweet soy sauce	1 clove garlic, crushed	finely chopped red chiles, to
2 tbsp tomato ketchup	4 tbsp corn oil	garnish
1 tsp rice wine vinegar		

1 Using a sharp knife, cut the salmon into slices. Place the slices of salmon in a shallow nonmetallic dish.

2 Mix together the soy sauce, tomato ketchup, rice wine vinegar, sugar, and garlic.

3 Pour the mixture over the salmon, toss well, and marinate for about 30 minutes.

4 Meanwhile, heat 3 tablespoons of the corn oil in a large preheated wok.

5 Add the leeks to the wok and stir-fry over a medium high heat for about 10 minutes, or until the leeks become crispy and tender.

6 Using a slotted spoon, carefully remove the leeks from the wok and transfer to warm serving plates.

7 Add the remaining oil to the wok. Add the salmon and the marinade to the wok and cook for 2 minutes. Spoon it over the leeks, garnish, and serve immediately.

VARIATION

You can use a fillet of beef instead of the salmon, if wished.

Stir-Fried Salmon with Pineapple

Serves 4

INGREDIENTS

1 cup baby corn cobs, halved	1 green bell pepper, seeded and sliced	½ cup bean sprouts
2 tbsp sunflower oil	1 pound salmon fillet, skin removed	2 tbsp tomato ketchup
1 red onion, sliced	1 tbsp paprika	2 tbsp soy sauce
1 orange bell pepper, seeded and sliced	8 ounce can cubed pineapple, drained	2 tbsp medium sherry
		1 tsp cornstarch

1 Using a sharp knife, cut the baby corn cobs in half.

2 Heat the sunflower oil in a large preheated wok. Add the onion, bell peppers, and baby corn cobs to the wok and stir-fry for 5 minutes.

3 Rinse the salmon fillet under cold running water and pat dry with absorbent paper towels.

4 Cut the salmon flesh into thin strips and place in a large bowl.

Sprinkle with the paprika and toss until well coated.

5 Add the salmon to the wok, together with the pineapple, and stir-fry for a further 2–3 minutes or until the fish is tender.

6 Add the bean sprouts to the wok and toss well.

7 Mix together the tomato ketchup, soy sauce, sherry, and cornstarch. Add the mixture to the wok and cook until the juices thicken. Transfer to

warm serving plates and serve immediately.

VARIATION

You can use trout fillets instead of the salmon as an alternative, if wished.

Tuna & Vegetable Stir-Fry

Serves 4

INGREDIENTS

3–4 medium carrots	1 pound fresh tuna	2 tbsp sherry
2 tbsp corn oil	2 tbsp fish sauce	1 tsp cornstarch
1 onion, sliced	1 tbsp palm sugar or brown sugar	rice or noodles, to serve
2½ cups snow peas	finely grated zest and juice of	
1¾ cups baby corn cobs, halved	1 orange	

1 Using a sharp knife, cut the carrots into thin sticks.

2 Heat the corn oil in a large preheated wok.

3 Add the onion, carrots, snow peas, and baby corn cobs to the wok and stir-fry for 5 minutes.

4 Using a sharp knife, thinly slice the tuna.

5 Add the tuna to the wok and stir-fry for 2–3 minutes, or until the tuna turns opaque.

6 Mix together the fish sauce, palm or brown sugar, orange zest and juice, sherry, and cornstarch.

7 Pour the mixture over the tuna and vegetables and cook for 2 minutes, or until the juices thicken. Serve with rice or noodles.

VARIATION

Try using swordfish steaks instead of the tuna. Swordfish steaks are now widely available and are similar in texture to tuna.

COOK'S TIP

Baby corn cobs have a deliciously sweet fragrance and flavor. They are available both fresh and canned.

Stir-Fried Cod with Mango

Serves 4

INGREDIENTS

2–3 medium carrots	1 green bell pepper, seeded and	1 tbsp soy sauce
2 tbsp vegetable oil	sliced	1⅓ cup tropical fruit juice
1 red onion, sliced	1 pound skinless cod fillet	1 tbsp lime juice
1 red bell pepper, seeded and	1 ripe mango	1 tbsp chopped cilantro
sliced	1 tsp cornstarch	

1 Using a sharp knife, slice the carrots into thin sticks.

2 Heat the vegetable oil in a preheated wok.

3 Add the onions, carrots, and bell peppers to the wok and stir-fry for 5 minutes.

4 Using a sharp knife, cut the cod into small cubes.

5 Peel the mango, then carefully remove the flesh from the central pit. Cut the flesh into thin slices.

6 Add the cod and mango to the wok and stir-fry for a further 4–5 minutes, or until the fish is cooked through. Do not stir the mixture too much or you may break the fish up.

7 Mix the cornstarch, soy sauce, fruit juice, and lime juice in a small bowl.

8 Pour the cornstarch mixture over the stir-fry and allow the mixture to bubble and the juices to thicken. Scatter with cilantro, transfer to a warm serving dish, and serve immediately.

VARIATION

You can use papaya as an alternative to the mango, if wished.

Stir-Fried Gingered Monkfish

Serves 4

INGREDIENTS

1 pound monkfish	1 tbsp corn oil	3 scallions, sliced
1 tbsp freshly grated ginger root	1 cup fine asparagus	1 tsp sesame oil
2 tbsp sweet chili sauce		

1 Using a sharp knife, slice the monkfish into thin flat rounds.

2 Mix the ginger with the chilli sauce in a small bowl.

3 Brush the ginger and chilli sauce mixture over the monkfish pieces.

4 Heat the corn oil in a large preheated wok.

5 Add the monkfish, asparagus and spring onions (scallions) to the wok and stir-fry for about 5 minutes.

6 Remove the wok from the heat, drizzle the sesame oil over the stir-fry and toss well to combine.

7 Transfer to warm serving plates and serve immediately.

VARIATION

Monkfish is quite expensive, but it is well worth using as it has a wonderful flavor and texture. Otherwise, could use cubes of chunky cod fillet instead.

COOK'S TIP

Some recipes specify to grate ginger before it is cooked with other ingredients. To do this, just peel the flesh and rub it at a 45 degree angle up and down on the fine section of a metal grater, or use a special wooden or ceramic ginger grater.

Braised Fish Fillets

Serves 4

INGREDIENTS

3–4 small Chinese dried mushrooms	2 scallions, finely chopped	1 tbsp light soy sauce
10½–12 ounces fish fillets	1 garlic clove, finely chopped	1 tsp rice wine or dry sherry
1 tsp salt	½ small green bell pepper, seeded and cut into small cubes	1 tbsp chili bean sauce
½ egg white, lightly beaten	½ small carrot, thinly sliced	2–3 tbsp Chinese stock or water
1 tsp cornstarch paste	½ cup canned sliced bamboo shoots, rinsed and drained	a few drops of sesame oil
2½ cups vegetable oil	½ tsp sugar	
1 tsp finely chopped ginger root		

1 Soak the dried mushrooms in a bowl of warm water for 30 minutes. Drain the mushrooms thoroughly on paper towels, reserving the soaking water for stock or soup. Squeeze the mushrooms to extract all of the moisture, cut off and discard any hard stems, and slice the caps thinly.

2 Cut the fish into bite-size pieces, then place in a shallow dish, and mix with a pinch of salt, the egg white, and cornstarch paste, turning the fish to coat well.

3 Heat the oil in a preheated wok. Add the fish pieces to the wok and deep-fry for about 1 minute. Remove the fish pieces with a slotted spoon and drain on paper towels.

4 Pour off the excess oil, leaving about 1 tablespoon in the wok. Add the ginger, scallions, and garlic to flavor the oil for a few seconds, then add the bell pepper, carrots, and bamboo shoots and stir-fry for about 1 minute.

5 Add the sugar, soy sauce, wine, chili bean sauce, stock or water, and the remaining salt and bring to a boil. Add the fish pieces, stir to coat well with the sauce, and braise for 1 minute.

6 Sprinkle with sesame oil, transfer to a warm serving dish, and serve immediately.

Fried Fish with Coconut & Basil

Serves 4

INGREDIENTS

2 tbsp vegetable oil	2 tbsp red Thai curry paste	175 g/6 oz cherry tomatoes,
450 g/1 lb skinless cod fillet	1 tbsp fish sauce	halved
25 g/1 oz/¼ cup seasoned flour	300 ml/½ pint/1¼ cups coconut	20 fresh basil leaves
1 clove garlic, crushed	milk	fragrant rice, to serve

1 Heat the vegetable oil in a large preheated wok.

2 Using a sharp knife, cut the fish into large cubes, taking care to remove any bones with a pair of tweezers.

3 Place the seasoned flour in a bowl. Add the cubes of fish and mix until well coated.

4 Add the coated fish to the wok and stir-fry over a high heat for 3–4 minutes, or until the fish just begins to brown at the edges.

5 Mix together the garlic, curry paste, fish sauce, and coconut milk in a bowl. Pour the mixture over the fish and bring to a boil.

6 Add the tomatoes to the mixture in the wok and simmer for 5 minutes.

7 Roughly chop or tear the fresh basil leaves. Add the basil to the wok, stir carefully to combine, taking care not to break up the cubes of fish.

8 Transfer to serving plates and serve hot with fragrant rice.

COOK'S TIP

Take care not to overcook the dish once the tomatoes are added, otherwise they will break down and the skins will come away.

Coconut Shrimp

Serves 4

INGREDIENTS

½ cup shredded coconut	½ tsp salt	1 pound fan-tail shrimp
½ cup fresh white bread crumbs	finely grated zest of 1 lime	sunflower or corn oil, for frying
1 tsp Chinese five-spice powder	1 egg white	lemon wedges, to garnish

1 Put the shredded coconut, white bread crumbs, Chinese five-spice powder, salt, and finely grated lime zest into a medium-size bowl and thoroughly mix together.

2 Lightly beat the egg white in a separate bowl.

3 Rinse the shrimp under cold running water and pat dry with absorbent paper towels.

4 Dip the shrimp into the egg white, then into the coconut crumb mixture, so that they are evenly coated.

5 Heat about 2 inches of sunflower or corn oil in a large preheated wok.

6 Add the shrimp to the wok and stir-fry for about 5 minutes or until golden colored and crispy.

7 Remove the shrimp with a slotted spoon, transfer to absorbent paper towels, and let drain thoroughly.

8 Transfer the coconut shrimp to warm serving dishes and garnish with lemon wedges. Serve immediately.

COOK'S TIP

Serve the prawns (shrimp) with a soy sauce or chilli sauce, if you wish.

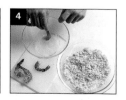

Shrimp Omelet

Serves 4

INGREDIENTS

2 tbsp sunflower oil	½ cup bean sprouts	1 tbsp light soy sauce
4 scallions, sliced	1 tsp cornstarch	6 eggs
12 ounces peeled shrimp		

1 Heat the sunflower oil in a large preheated wok.

2 Using a sharp knife, trim the scallions and cut them into thin slices.

3 Add the shrimp, scallions, and bean sprouts to the wok and stir-fry for 2 minutes.

4 Mix together the cornstarch and soy sauce in a small bowl.

5 Beat together the eggs and 3 tablespoons of cold water and then blend with the cornstarch and soy mixture.

6 Add the egg mixture to the wok and cook for about 5–6 minutes, or until the mixture is just setting.

7 Transfer the omelet to a serving plate and cut into quarters to serve.

VARIATION

Add any other vegetables of your choice, such as grated carrot or cooked peas, to the omelet in step 3, if you wish.

COOK'S TIP

It is important to use fresh bean sprouts for this dish as the canned ones don't have the crunchy texture necessary.

Shrimp with Spicy Tomatoes

Serves 4

INGREDIENTS

2 tbsp corn oil
1 onion
2 cloves garlic, crushed
1 tsp cumin seeds

1 tbsp sugar
14 ounce can chopped tomatoes
1 tbsp sun-dried tomato paste

1 tbsp chopped fresh basil
1 pound peeled jumbo shrimp
salt and pepper

1 Heat the corn oil in a large preheated wok.

2 Using a sharp knife, finely chop the onion.

3 Add the onion and garlic to the wok and stir-fry for 2–3 minutes, or until softened.

4 Stir in the cumin seeds and stir-fry for 1 minute.

5 Add the sugar, chopped tomatoes, and sun-dried tomato paste to the wok. Bring the mixture to a boil, then reduce the heat and simmer the sauce for about 10 minutes.

6 Add the basil, shrimp, and salt and pepper to taste to the mixture in the wok. Increase the heat and cook for a further 2–3 minutes or until the shrimp are completely cooked through.

COOK'S TIP

Always heat your wok before you add oil or other ingredients. This will prevent anything from sticking to it.

COOK'S TIP

Sun-dried tomato paste has a much more intense flavor than that of normal tomato paste. It adds a distinctive intensity to any tomato-based dish.

Shrimp with Crispy Ginger

Serves 4

INGREDIENTS

2 -inch piece fresh ginger root	½ cup frozen peas	1 tsp Chinese five-spice powder
oil, for frying	½ cup bean sprouts	1 tbsp tomato paste
1 onion, diced	1 pound peeled jumbo shrimp	1 tbsp soy sauce
3–4 medium carrots, diced		

1 Using a sharp knife, peel the ginger and slice it into very thin sticks.

2 Heat about 1 inch of oil in a large preheated wok.

3 Add the ginger to the wok and stir-fry for 1 minute, or until the ginger is crispy. Remove the ginger with a slotted spoon and let drain on absorbent paper towels. Set aside.

4 Drain all of the oil from the wok except for about 2 tablespoons.

5 Add the onions and carrots to the wok and stir-fry for 5 minutes.

6 Add the peas and bean sprouts to the wok and stir-fry for 2 minutes.

7 Rinse the shrimp under cold running water and pat dry thoroughly with absorbent paper towels.

8 Mix together the five-spice powder, tomato paste, and soy sauce. Brush the mixture all over the shrimp.

9 Add the shrimp to the wok and stir-fry for a further 2 minutes, or until the shrimp are completely cooked through. Transfer the shrimp mixture to a warm serving bowl and top with the reserved crispy ginger. Serve immediately.

VARIATION

Use slices of white fish instead of the shrimp as an alternative, if you wish.

258

Vegetables with Shrimp & Egg

Serves 4

INGREDIENTS

8 ounces zucchini	1 onion, sliced	pinch of Chinese five-spice
3 tbsp vegetable oil	³/₄ cup bean sprouts	powder
2 eggs	8 ounces peeled shrimp	¹/₄ cup peanuts, chopped
3–4 medium carrots, grated	2 tbsp soy sauce	2 tbsp fresh chopped cilantro

1 Trim and finely grate the zucchini.

2 Heat 1 tablespoon of the oil in a large preheated wok.

3 Lightly beat the eggs with 2 tablespoons of cold water. Pour the mixture into the wok and cook for 2–3 minutes or until the egg sets.

4 Remove the omelet from the wok and transfer to a clean board. Fold the omelet, cut it into thin strips, and set aside until it is required.

5 Add the remaining oil to the wok. Add the carrots, onion, and zucchini and stir-fry for 5 minutes.

6 Add the bean sprouts and shrimp to the wok and cook for a further 2 minutes, or until the shrimp are completely heated through.

7 Add the soy sauce, five-spice powder and peanuts to the wok, together with the strips of omelet, and heat through. Garnish with chopped fresh cilantro and serve immediately.

COOK'S TIP

The water is mixed with the egg in step 3 for a lighter, less rubbery omelet.

Stir-Fried Crab Claws with Chili

Serves 4

INGREDIENTS

1 pound 9 ounces crab claws	3 red chiles, seeded and	1¼ cups fish stock
1 tbsp corn oil	finely chopped	1 tbsp cornstarch
2 cloves garlic, crushed	2 tbsp sweet chili sauce	salt and pepper
1 tbsp grated fresh ginger root	3 tbsp tomato ketchup	1 tbsp fresh chives, snipped

1 Gently crack the crab claws with a nut cracker. This process will allow the flavors of the chili, garlic, and ginger to fully penetrate the crab meat.

2 Heat the corn oil in a large preheated wok.

3 Add the crab claws to the wok and stir-fry for about 5 minutes.

4 Add the garlic, ginger, and chiles to the wok and stir-fry for 1 minute, tossing the crab claws to coat all over.

5 Mix together the chili sauce, tomato ketchup, fish stock, and cornstarch in a small bowl.

6 Add the chili and cornstarch mixture to the wok and cook, stirring occasionally, until the sauce starts to thicken. Season with salt and pepper to taste.

7 Transfer the crab claws and chili sauce to warm serving dishes and garnish with plenty of snipped fresh chives. Serve immediately.

COOK'S TIP

If crab claws are not easily available, use a whole crab, cut into eight pieces, instead.

Chinese Leaves with Shiitake Mushrooms & Crab Meat

Serves 4

INGREDIENTS

8 ounces shiitake mushrooms
2 tbsp vegetable oil
2 cloves garlic, crushed
6 scallions, sliced

1 head Chinese cabbage, shredded
1 tbsp mild curry paste
6 tbsp coconut milk
7 ounce can white crab meat,

drained
1 tsp chili flakes

1 Using a sharp knife, cut the the mushrooms into slices.

2 Heat the vegetable oil in a large preheated wok.

3 Add the mushrooms and garlic to the wok and stir-fry for 3 minutes, or until the mushrooms have softened.

4 Add the scallions and shredded Chinese cabbage to the wok and stir-fry until the leaves have wilted.

5 Mix together the mild curry paste and coconut milk in a small bowl.

6 Add the curry paste and coconut milk mixture to the wok, together with the crab meat and chili flakes. Mix together until thoroughly combined and heat through until the juices start to bubble.

7 Transfer to warm serving bowls and then serve immediately.

COOK'S TIP

Shiitake mushrooms are now readily available in the fresh vegetable section of most large supermarkets.

Stir-Fried Lettuce with Mussels & Lemon Grass

Serves 4

INGREDIENTS

2¼ pounds mussels in their shells, scrubbed and debearded	2 tbsp lemon juice	1 iceberg lettuce
2 stalks lemon grass, thinly sliced	½ cup water	finely grated zest of 1 lemon
	2 tbsp butter	2 tbsp oyster sauce

1 Discard any mussels that do not shut when sharply tapped. Place the mussels in a large saucepan.

2 Add the lemon grass, lemon juice, and water to the pan, cover, and cook for 5 minutes, or until the mussels have opened. Discard any that have not opened.

3 Carefully remove the cooked mussels from their shells.

4 Heat the butter in a large preheated wok.

5 Add the lettuce and lemon zest to the wok and stir-fry for 2 minutes, or until the lettuce begins to wilt.

6 Add the oyster sauce to the mixture in the wok, stir, and heat through. Serve immediately.

COOK'S TIP

Lemon grass with its citrus fragrance and lemon flavor looks like a fibrous scallion and is often used in Thai cooking.

COOK'S TIP

When using fresh mussels, be sure to discard any opened mussels before scrubbing and any unopened mussels after cooking.

Mussels in Black Bean Sauce with Spinach

Serves 4

INGREDIENTS

12 ounces leeks

12 ounces cooked green-lipped mussels, shelled

1 tsp cumin seeds

2 tbsp vegetable oil

2 cloves garlic, crushed

1 red bell pepper, seeded and sliced

3/4 cup canned bamboo shoots, drained

6 ounces baby spinach

5 3/4 ounce jar black bean sauce

1 Using a sharp knife, trim the leeks and shred them.

2 Place the mussels in a large bowl, sprinkle with the cumin seeds, and toss well to coat all over.

3 Heat the vegetable oil in a large preheated wok.

4 Add the leeks, garlic, and red bell pepper to the wok and stir-fry for 5 minutes, or until the vegetables are tender.

5 Add the bamboo shoots, baby spinach leaves, and cooked green-lipped mussels to the wok and stir-fry for about 2 minutes.

6 Pour the black bean sauce over the ingredients in the wok, toss well to coat all over, and simmer for a few seconds, stirring occasionally.

7 Transfer the stir-fry to warm serving bowls and serve immediately.

COOK'S TIP

If fresh green-lipped mussels are not available, they can be bought shelled in cans and jars from most large supermarkets.

Scallop Pancakes

Serves 4

INGREDIENTS

³/₄ cup fine green beans	1 egg	1 tbsp fish sauce
1 red chili	3 scallions, sliced	oil, for frying
1 pound scallops, without corals	½ cup rice flour	sweet chili dip, to serve

1 Using a sharp knife, trim the green beans and slice them very thinly.

2 Using a sharp knife, seed and very finely chop the red chili.

3 Bring a small saucepan of lightly salted water to a boil. Add the green beans to the pan and cook for 3–4 minutes, or until just softened.

4 Roughly chop the scallops and place them in a large bowl. Add the cooked beans to the scallops.

5 Mix the egg with the scallions, rice flour, fish sauce, and chili until thoroughly combined. Add to the scallops and mix well.

6 Heat about 1 inch of oil in a large preheated wok. Add a ladleful of the mixture to the wok and cook for 5 minutes, until golden and set. Remove the pancake from the wok and let drain on absorbent paper towels. Repeat with the remaining pancake mixture.

7 Serve the pancakes hot with a sweet chili dip.

VARIATION

You could use shrimp or shelled clams instead of the scallops, if wished. You could use prawns (shrimp) or shelled clams instead of the scallops, if you prefer.

Seared Scallops with Butter Sauce

Serves 4

INGREDIENTS

1 pound scallops, without corals	2 tbsp vegetable oil	3 tbsp sweet soy sauce
6 scallions	1 green chili, seeded and sliced	2 tbsp butter, diced

1 Rinse the scallops well under cold running water, then pat the scallops dry with absorbent paper towels.

2 Using a sharp knife, slice each scallop in half horizontally.

3 Using a sharp knife, trim and thinly slice the scallions.

4 Heat the vegetable oil in a large preheated wok.

5 Add the sliced chili, scallions, and scallops to the wok and stir-fry over a high heat for about 4–5 minutes, or until the scallops are just cooked through and have become slightly opaque.

6 Add the soy sauce and butter to the scallop stir-fry and heat through until the butter melts.

COOK'S TIP

If you buy scallops on the shell, slide a knife underneath the membrane to loosen and cut off the tough muscle that holds the scallop to the shell. Discard the black stomach sac and intestinal vein.

COOK'S TIP

Use frozen scallops if desired, but make sure they are completely thawed before cooking. In addition, do not overcook them, as they will easily disintegrate.

7 Transfer to warm serving bowls and serve hot.

Stir-Fried Oysters with Bean Curd, Lemon, & Cilantro

Serves 4

INGREDIENTS

8 ounces leeks	2 tbsp fresh lemon juice	⅓ cup fish stock
12 ounces bean curd	1 tsp cornstarch	2 tbsp chopped fresh cilantro
2 tbsp sunflower oil	2 tbsp light soy sauce	1 tsp finely grated lemon zest
12 ounces shelled oysters		

1 Using a sharp knife, trim and slice the leeks.

2 Cut the bean curd into bite-size pieces.

3 Heat the sunflower oil in a large preheated wok.

4 Add the leeks to the wok and stir-fry for about 2 minutes.

5 Add the bean curd and oysters to the wok and stir-fry for 1–2 minutes.

6 Mix together the lemon juice, cornstarch, light soy sauce, and fish stock to a smooth paste in a small bowl.

7 Pour the cornstarch mixture into the wok and cook, stirring occasionally, until the juices start to thicken.

8 Transfer the stir-fry to warm serving bowls and scatter the chopped cilantro and grated lemon zest on top. Serve the stir-fry immediately.

VARIATION

Shelled clams or mussels could be used instead of the oysters, if wished.

Crispy Fried Squid with Salt & Pepper

Serves 4

INGREDIENTS

1 pound squid, cleaned	1 tsp freshly ground black pepper	peanut oil, for frying
4 tbsp cornstarch	1 tsp chili flakes	dipping sauce, to serve
1 tsp salt		

1 Using a sharp knife, remove the tentacles from the squid and trim. Slice the bodies down one side and open out to give a flat piece.

2 Score the flat pieces with a criss-cross pattern, then cut each piece into 4.

3 Mix together the cornstarch, salt, pepper, and chili flakes.

4 Place the salt and pepper mixture in a large plastic bag. Add the squid pieces, tie the top tightly, and shake the bag thoroughly to coat the squid well in the flour mixture.

5 Heat about 2 inches of peanut oil in a large preheated wok.

6 Add the squid pieces to the wok and stir-fry, in batches, for about 2 minutes, or until the squid pieces start to curl up. Do not overcook or the squid will become tough.

7 Remove the squid pieces with a slotted spoon, transfer to absorbent paper towels, and drain thoroughly.

8 Transfer to serving plates and serve immediately with a dipping sauce.

COOK'S TIP

Squid tubes may be purchased frozen if they are not available fresh. They are usually ready-cleaned and are easy to use. Ensure that they are completely thawed before cooking.

Stir-Fried Squid with Green Bell Peppers & Black Bean Sauce

Serves 4

INGREDIENTS

1 pound squid rings
2 tbsp all-purpose flour
$\frac{1}{2}$ tsp salt

1 green bell pepper
2 tbsp peanut oil

1 red onion, sliced
$5\frac{3}{4}$ ounce jar black bean sauce

1 Rinse the squid rings under cold running water and pat dry with absorbent paper towels.

2 Place the all-purpose flour and salt in a bowl and mix together. Add the squid rings and toss until they are finely coated.

3 Using a sharp knife, seed the bell pepper. Slice the bell pepper into thin strips.

4 Heat the peanut oil in a large preheated wok.

5 Add the bell pepper and red onion to the wok and stir-fry for about 2 minutes, or until the vegetables are just beginning to soften.

6 Add the squid rings to the wok and cook for a further 5 minutes, or until the squid is cooked through.

7 Add the black bean sauce to the wok and heat through until the juices are bubbling. Transfer to warm serving bowls and serve immediately.

COOK'S TIP

Serve this recipe with fried rice or noodles tossed in soy sauce, if you wish.

Steamed Fish with Black Bean Sauce

Serves 4

INGREDIENTS

2 pounds whole snapper, cleaned and scaled	2 tsp sesame oil	1 small leek, shredded
3 garlic cloves, crushed	2 tbsp light soy sauce	1 small red bell pepper, seeded and cut into thin strips
2 tbsp black bean sauce	2 tsp superfine sugar	shredded leek and lemon wedges, to garnish
1 tsp cornstarch	2 tbsp Chinese rice wine or dry sherry	boiled rice or noodles, to serve

1 Rinse the fish inside and out with cold running water and pat dry with paper towels. Make 2-3 diagonal slashes in the flesh on each side of the fish, using a sharp knife. Rub the garlic into the fish.

2 Thoroughly mix the black bean sauce, cornstarch, sesame oil, light soy sauce, sugar, and Chinese rice wine or dry sherry together in a bowl. Place the fish in a shallow heatproof dish and pour the sauce mixture over the top.

3 Sprinkle the leek and bell pepper strips on top of the sauce. Place the dish in the top of a steamer, cover, and steam for 10 minutes, or until the fish is cooked through. Transfer to a serving dish, garnish with shredded leek and lemon wedges, and serve with rice or noodles.

VARIATION

Whole sea bream or sea bass may be used in this recipe instead of snapper, if desired.

COOK'S TIP

Insert the point of a sharp knife into the fish to test if it is cooked. The fish is cooked through if the knife goes into the flesh easily.

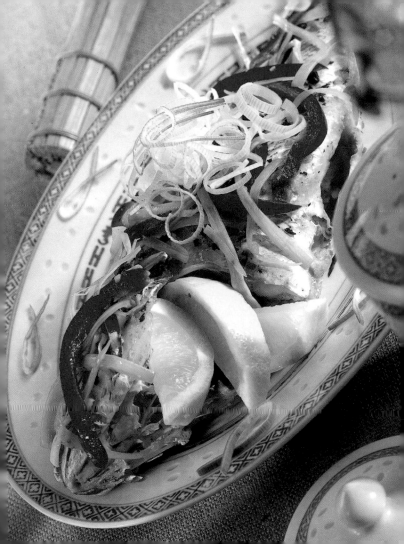

Steamed Snapper with Fruit & Ginger Stuffing

Serves 4

INGREDIENTS

3 pounds whole snapper, cleaned
and scaled
6 ounces fresh spinach
orange slices and shredded
scallion, to garnish

STUFFING:
2 cups cooked long grain rice
1 tsp grated fresh ginger root
2 scallions, finely chopped
2 tsp light soy sauce

1 tsp sesame oil
½ tsp ground star anise
1 orange, segmented and
chopped, and shredded
scallion, to garnish

1 Rinse the fish inside and out under cold running water and pat dry with paper towels. Blanch the spinach for 40 seconds, rinse in cold water, and drain well, pressing out as much moisture as possible. Arrange the spinach on a heatproof plate and place the fish on top.

2 To make the stuffing, mix together the cooked rice, grated ginger, scallion, soy sauce, sesame oil, and star anise in a large bowl.

3 Spoon the stuffing into the body cavity of the fish, pressing it in well with a spoon.

4 Cover the plate and cook in a steamer for 10 minutes, or until the fish is cooked through. Carefully transfer the fish to a warm serving dish, garnish with orange slices and shredded scallion, and serve immediately.

COOK'S TIP

The name snapper covers a family of tropical and subtropical fish that vary in color. They may be red, orange, pink, red, gray, or blue-green. Some are striped or spotted and they range in size from about 6 inches to 3 feet.

Trout with Pineapple

Serves 4

INGREDIENTS

4 trout fillets, skinned

2 tbsp vegetable oil

2 garlic cloves, cut into slivers

4 slices fresh pineapple, peeled and diced

1 celery stalk, sliced

1 tbsp light soy sauce

¼ cup fresh or unsweetened pineapple juice

⅔ cup fish stock

1 tsp cornstarch

2 tsp water

shredded celery leaves and fresh red chili strips, to garnish

1 Cut the trout fillets into strips. Heat 1 tablespoon of the vegetable oil in a preheated wok until almost smoking. Reduce the heat slightly, add the fish, and sauté for 2 minutes. Remove from the wok and set aside.

2 Add the remaining oil to the wok, reduce the heat, and add the garlic, pineapple, and celery. Stir-fry for 1–2 minutes.

3 Add the soy sauce, pineapple juice, and fish stock to the wok. Bring to a boil and cook, stirring, for 2–3 minutes, or until the sauce has reduced.

4 Blend the cornstarch with the water to form a smooth paste and stir it into the wok. Bring the sauce to a boil and cook, stirring constantly, until the sauce has thickened and cleared.

5 Return the fish to the wok, and cook, stirring gently, until heated through. Transfer to a warm serving dish and serve, garnished with shredded celery leaves and red chili strips.

COOK'S TIP

Use canned pineapple instead of fresh pineapple if desired, choosing slices in unsweetened, natural juice instead of syrup.

Mullet with Ginger

Serves 4

INGREDIENTS

1 whole mullet, cleaned and scaled
2 scallions, chopped
1 tsp grated fresh ginger root
$\frac{1}{2}$ cup garlic wine vinegar

$\frac{1}{2}$ cup light soy sauce
3 tsp superfine sugar
dash of chili sauce
$\frac{1}{2}$ cup fish stock

1 green bell pepper, seeded and
    thinly sliced
1 large tomato, peeled, seeded,
    and cut into thin strips
salt and pepper
sliced tomato, to garnish

1 Rinse the fish inside and out and pat thoroughly dry with paper towels.

2 Make 3 diagonal slits in the flesh on each side of the fish. Season with salt and pepper inside and out.

3 Place the fish on a heatproof plate and scatter the chopped scallions and grated ginger over the top. Cover and steam for 10 minutes, or

until the fish is cooked through.

4 Meanwhile, place the garlic wine vinegar, soy sauce, sugar, chili sauce, fish stock, bell pepper, and tomato in a saucepan and bring to a boil, stirring occasionally. Cook over a high heat until the sauce has slightly reduced and thickened.

5 Remove the fish from the steamer and

transfer to a warm serving dish. Pour the sauce over the fish, garnish with tomato slices, and serve immediately.

COOK'S TIP

Use fillets of fish for this recipe if desired, and reduce the cooking time to 5–7 minutes.

Szechwan White Fish

Serves 4

INGREDIENTS

12 ounces white fish fillets	½-inch piece fresh ginger root,	½ tsp ground Szechwan pepper
1 small egg, beaten	finely chopped	¾ cup fish stock
3 tbsp all-purpose flour	1 onion, finely chopped	1 tsp superfine sugar
4 tbsp dry white wine	1 celery stalk, chopped	1 tsp cornstarch
3 tbsp light soy sauce	1 fresh red chili, chopped	2 tsp water
vegetable oil, for frying	3 scallions, chopped	chili flowers and celery leaves,
1 garlic clove, cut into slivers	1 tsp rice wine vinegar	to garnish

1 Cut the fish fillets into 1½-inch cubes.

2 In a mixing bowl, beat together the egg, flour, wine, and 1 tablespoon of soy sauce to make a batter.

3 Dip the cubes of fish into the batter to coat well.

4 Heat the oil in a preheated wok until it is almost smoking. Reduce the heat slightly and cook the fish, in batches, for 2–3 minutes, until golden brown. Drain on paper towels, set aside, and keep warm.

5 Carefully pour all but 1 tablespoon of the oil from the wok and return to the heat. Add the garlic, ginger, onion, celery, chili, and scallions and stir-fry for 1–2 minutes.

6 Stir in the remaining soy sauce and the vinegar.

7 Add the Szechwan pepper, fish stock, and sugar to the wok. Blend the cornstarch with the water to form a smooth paste and stir it into the stock. Bring to a boil and cook until the sauce thickens and clears.

8 Return the fish to the wok and cook for 1–2 minutes, until thoroughly heated through. Transfer to a serving dish, garnish with chili flowers and celery leaves, and serve.

Crispy Fish

Serves 4

INGREDIENTS

1 pound white fish fillets	4 tbsp milk	pinch of chili powder
	vegetable oil, for deep-frying	3 tbsp tomato paste
BATTER:		1 tbsp rice wine vinegar
1/2 cup all-purpose flour	SAUCE:	2 tbsp dark soy sauce
1 egg, separated	1 fresh red chili, chopped	2 tbsp Chinese rice wine
1 tbsp peanut oil	2 garlic cloves, crushed	2 tbsp water
		pinch of superfine sugar

1 Cut the fish into 1-inch cubes and set aside. Sift the flour into a mixing bowl and make a well in the center. Add the egg yolk and oil to the bowl and gradually stir in the milk, incorporating the flour to form a smooth batter. Let stand for 20 minutes.

2 Beat the egg white until it forms peaks, and fold it into the batter. Heat the oil in a preheated wok. Dip the fish into the batter and fry, in batches, for 8–10 minutes, until cooked through. Remove the fish from the wok with a slotted spoon, set aside, and keep warm.

3 Pour off all but 1 tablespoon of oil from the wok and return to the heat. Add the chili, garlic, chili powder, tomato paste, rice wine vinegar, soy sauce, Chinese rice wine, water, and sugar and cook, stirring, for 3–4 minutes.

4 Return the fish to the wok and stir gently to coat it in the sauce. Cook for 2–3 minutes, until hot. Transfer the fish and sauce to a warm serving dish and serve immediately.

COOK'S TIP

Take care when pouring hot oil from the wok and ensure that you transfer it to a suitable bowl until cool.

Seafood Medley

Serves 4

INGREDIENTS

2 tbsp dry white wine
1 egg white, lightly beaten
½ tsp Chinese five-spice powder
1 tsp cornstarch
10½ ounces raw shrimp, peeled and deveined

4½ ounces prepared squid, cut into rings
4½ ounces white fish fillets, cut into strips
vegetable oil, for deep-frying

1 green bell pepper, seeded and cut into thin strips
1 carrot, peeled and cut into thin strips
4 baby corncobs, halved lengthwise

1 Mix together the wine, egg white, Chinese five-spice powder, and cornstarch in a large bowl, combining well. Add the shrimp, squid rings, and fish fillets and stir gently to coat thoroughly and evenly. Remove the fish and seafood with a slotted spoon, reserving any leftover wine and cornstarch mixture.

2 Heat the oil in a preheated wok. Add the shrimp, squid, and fish strips and deep-fry for 2–3 minutes. Remove the seafood mixture from the wok with a slotted spoon and set aside.

3 Pour off all but 1 tablespoon of oil from the wok and return to the heat. Add the bell pepper, carrot, and corncobs and stir-fry for 4–5 minutes.

4 Return the seafood mixture to the wok and add any remaining wine and cornstarch mixture. Cook, stirring well to heat through. Transfer to a serving plate and serve immediately.

COOK'S TIP

Open up the squid rings and, using a sharp knife, score a lattice pattern on the flesh to make them look attractive.

Fried Shrimp with Cashews

Serves 4

INGREDIENTS

2 garlic cloves, crushed	1 leek, sliced	SAUCE:
1 tbsp cornstarch	4½ ounces broccoli florets	¾ cup fish stock
pinch of superfine sugar	1 orange bell pepper, seeded	1 tbsp cornstarch
1 pound raw jumbo shrimp	and diced	dash of chili sauce
4 tbsp vegetable oil	¾ cup unsalted cashew nuts	2 tsp sesame oil
		1 tbsp Chinese rice wine

1 Mix together the garlic, cornstarch, and sugar in a large bowl. Peel and devein the jumbo shrimp. Stir the shrimp into the cornstarch mixture to coat thoroughly.

2 Heat the oil in a preheated wok and add the shrimp mixture. Stir-fry over a high heat for 20–30 seconds, until the shrimp turn pink. Remove the shrimp from the wok with a slotted spoon, drain on paper towels, and set aside.

3 Add the leek, broccoli, and bell pepper to the wok and stir-fry for 2 minutes.

4 To make the sauce, mix together the fish stock, cornstarch, chili sauce to taste, the sesame oil, and Chinese rice wine. Add the mixture to the wok, together with the cashews. Return the shrimp to the wok and cook, stirring frequently, for 1 minute to heat through completely. Transfer to a warm serving dish and serve immediately.

VARIATION

This recipe also works well with chicken, pork, or beef strips instead of the shrimp. Use 8 ounces meat instead of 1 pound shrimp.

Shrimp Fu Yong

Serves 4

INGREDIENTS

2 tbsp vegetable oil
1 carrot, peeled and grated
5 eggs, beaten
8 ounces raw small shrimp, peeled

1 tbsp light soy sauce
pinch of Chinese five-spice powder

2 scallions, chopped
2 tsp sesame seeds
1 tsp sesame oil

1 Heat the vegetable oil in a preheated wok.

2 Add the carrot and stir-fry for 1 2 minutes.

3 Push the carrot to one side of the wok and add the eggs. Cook, stirring gently, for 1–2 minutes.

4 Stir the small shrimp, soy sauce, and five-spice powder into the mixture in the wok. Stir-fry the mixture for 2–3 minutes, or until the small shrimp have changed color and the mixture is almost dry.

5 Turn the shrimp fu yong out onto a warm serving plate and sprinkle the scallions, sesame seeds, and sesame oil on top. Serve immediately.

VARIATION

For a more substantial dish, you could add 1 cup cooked long-grain rice with the small shrimp in step 4. Taste and adjust the quantities of soy sauce, Chinese five-spice powder, and sesame oil if necessary. This is a useful way of using up leftover rice.

COOK'S TIP

If only cooked prawns (shrimp) are available, add them just before the end of cooking, but make sure that they are fully incorporated into the fu yong. They require only heating through— overcooking will make them chewy and tasteless.

Cantonese Shrimp

Serves 4

INGREDIENTS

5 tbsp vegetable oil
4 garlic cloves, crushed
1½ pounds raw shrimp, shelled
  and deveined
2-inch piece fresh ginger root,
  chopped

6 ounces lean pork, diced
1 leek, sliced
3 eggs, beaten
shredded leek and red bell
  pepper matchsticks, to
  garnish

SAUCE:
2 tbsp dry sherry
2 tbsp light soy sauce
2 tsp superfine sugar
⅔ cup fish stock
4½ tsp cornstarch
3 tbsp water

1 Heat 2 tablespoons of the vegetable oil in a preheated wok. Add the garlic and stir-fry for about 30 seconds. Add the shrimp and stir-fry for 5 minutes, or until they change color. Remove the shrimp from the wok with a slotted spoon, drain, set aside, and keep warm.

2 Add the remaining oil to the wok and heat. Add the ginger, diced pork, and leek and stir-fry over a medium heat for 4-5 minutes, or until the pork is lightly colored and sealed.

3 Add the sherry, soy sauce, sugar, and fish stock to the wok. Blend the cornstarch with the water to form a smooth paste and stir it into the wok. Cook, stirring, until the sauce thickens and clears.

4 Return the shrimp to the wok and add the beaten eggs. Cook for 5–6 minutes, stirring occasionally, until the eggs set. Transfer to a warm serving dish, garnish with shredded leek and bell pepper matchsticks, and serve.

COOK'S TIP

If possible, use Chinese rice wine instead of the sherry.

Squid with Oyster Sauce

Serves 4

INGREDIENTS

1 pound squid	2 ounces snow peas	SAUCE:
²/₃ cup vegetable oil	5 tbsp hot fish stock	1 tbsp oyster sauce
½-inch piece fresh ginger root, grated	red bell pepper triangles, to garnish	1 tbsp light soy sauce
		pinch of superfine sugar
		1 garlic clove, crushed

1 To prepare the squid, cut down the center of the body lengthwise. Flatten the squid out, inside uppermost, and score a lattice design deep into the flesh, using a sharp knife.

2 To make the sauce, combine the oyster sauce, soy sauce, sugar, and garlic in a small bowl. Stir to dissolve the sugar and set aside until required.

3 Heat the vegetable oil in a preheated wok until almost smoking.

Lower the heat slightly, add the squid, and stir-fry until they curl up. Remove with a slotted spoon and drain thoroughly on paper towels.

4 Pour off all but 2 tablespoons of the oil and return the wok to the heat. Add the ginger and snow peas and stir-fry for about 1 minute.

5 Return the squid to the wok and pour in the sauce and hot fish stock. Simmer the mixture for about 3 minutes,

or until the liquid has thickened.

6 Transfer to a warm serving dish, garnish with bell pepper triangles, and serve immediately.

COOK'S TIP

Take care not to overcook the squid, otherwise it will be rubbery and unappetizing.

Scallops in Ginger Sauce

Serves 4

INGREDIENTS

2 tbsp vegetable oil
1 pound scallops, cleaned
and halved
1-inch piece fresh ginger root,
finely chopped

3 garlic cloves, crushed
2 leeks, shredded
3/4 cup shelled peas
4 1/2 ounces canned bamboo
shoots, drained and rinsed

2 tbsp light soy sauce
2 tbsp unsweetened orange juice
1 tsp superfine sugar
orange zest, to garnish

1 Heat the oil in a preheated wok. Add the scallops and stir-fry for 1–2 minutes. Remove the scallops from the wok with a slotted spoon and set aside.

2 Add the ginger and garlic to the wok and stir-fry for 30 seconds. Stir in the leeks and peas and cook, stirring, for a further 2 minutes.

3 Add the bamboo shoots and return the scallops to the wok. Stir gently to mix without breaking up the scallops.

4 Stir in the soy sauce, orange juice, and sugar and cook for 1–2 minutes. Transfer to a serving dish, garnish with the orange zest, and serve immediately.

COOK'S TIP

The edible parts of a scallop are the round white muscle and the orange and white coral or roe. The frilly skirt surrounding the muscle— the gills and mantle—may be used for making shellfish stock. All other parts should be discarded.

COOK'S TIP

Frozen scallops may be thawed and used in this recipe, adding them at the end of cooking to prevent them from breaking up. If you are buying scallops already shelled, check whether they are fresh or frozen. Fresh scallops are cream colored and more translucent, while frozen scallops tend to be pure white.

Crab in Ginger Sauce

Serves 4

INGREDIENTS

2 small cooked crabs	1 green bell pepper, seeded and	½ tsp sesame oil
2 tbsp vegetable oil	cut into thin strips	⅔ cup fish stock
3-inch piece fresh ginger root,	6 scallions, cut into 1-inch	1 tsp light brown sugar
grated	lengths	2 tsp cornstarch
2 garlic cloves, thinly sliced	2 tbsp dry sherry	⅔ cup water

1 Rinse the crabs and gently loosen around the shell at the top. Using a sharp knife, cut away the gray tissue and discard. Rinse the crabs again.

2 Twist off the legs and claws from the crabs. Using a pair of crab claw crackers or a cleaver, gently crack the claws to break through the shell to expose the flesh. Remove and discard any loose pieces of shell.

3 Separate the body and discard the inedible lungs and sac. Cut down the center of each crab to separate the body into two pieces and then cut each of these in half again.

4 Heat the oil in a preheated wok. Add the ginger and garlic and stir-fry for 1 minute. Add the crab pieces and stir-fry for 1 minute.

5 Stir in the bell pepper, scallions, sherry, sesame oil, stock, and sugar. Bring to a boil, reduce the heat, cover, and simmer for 3–4 minutes.

6 Blend the cornstarch with the water to make a smooth paste and stir it into the wok. Bring to a boil, stirring, until the sauce is thickened and clear. Transfer to a warm serving dish and serve immediately.

COOK'S TIP

If desired, remove the crab meat from the shells prior to stir-frying and add to the wok with the bell pepper.

Indonesian-Style Spicy Cod

Serves 4

INGREDIENTS

4 cod steaks	2 fresh red chiles, seeded	2 tbsp butter, cut into small cubes
1 stalk lemon grass	and chopped	8 tbsp canned coconut milk
1 small red onion, chopped	1 tsp grated fresh ginger root	2 tbsp lemon juice
3 cloves garlic, chopped	1/4 tsp turmeric	salt and pepper
		red chiles, to garnish (optional)

1 Rinse the cod steaks and pat them dry on absorbent paper towels.

2 Remove and discard the outer leaves from the lemon grass stalk and thinly slice the inner section.

3 Place the lemon grass, onion, garlic, chili, ginger, and turmeric in a food processor and blend until the ingredients are finely chopped. Season with salt and pepper to taste.

4 With the processor running, add the butter, coconut milk, and lemon juice and process until well blended.

5 Place the fish in a shallow, nonmetallic dish. Pour the coconut mixture on top and turn the fish until well coated.

6 If you have one, place the fish steaks in a hinged basket, which will make them easier to turn. Broil over hot coals for 15 minutes or until the fish is cooked through, turning once. Serve garnished with red chiles, if desired.

COOK'S TIP

If you prefer a milder flavor, omit the chiles altogether. For a hotter flavor do not remove the seeds from the chiles.

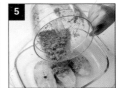

Salmon Yakitori

Serves 4

INGREDIENTS

12 ounces chunky salmon fillet
8 baby leeks
Yakitori sauce:

5 tbsp light soy sauce
5 tbsp fish stock
2 tbsp superfine sugar

5 tbsp dry white wine
3 tbsp sweet sherry
1 clove garlic, crushed

1 Skin the salmon and cut the flesh into 2-inch chunks. Trim the leeks and cut them into 2-inch lengths.

2 Thread the pieces of salmon and leek alternately onto 8 presoaked wooden skewers. Chill in the refrigerator until required.

3 To make the sauce, place all of the ingredients in a small pan and heat gently, stirring, until the sugar dissolves. Bring to a boil, then reduce the heat, and simmer for 2 minutes. Strain the sauce and leave to cool.

4 Pour about one-third of the sauce into a dish and then set aside to serve with the kabobs.

5 Brush plenty of the remaining sauce over the skewers and cook directly on the rack or, if preferred, place a sheet of greased foil on the rack and cook the salmon on that. Broil the skewers over hot coals for about 10 minutes, turning once. Baste the skewers frequently during

cooking with the remaining sauce to prevent the fish and vegetables from drying out.

6 Serve the kabobs with the dish of reserved sauce for dipping.

COOK'S TIP

Soak the wooden skewers in cold water for at least 30 minutes to prevent them from burning during cooking. You can make the kabobs and sauce several hours ahead of time. Refrigerate until required.

Japanese-Style Charbroiled Flounder

Serves 4

INGREDIENTS

4 small flounders
6 tbsp soy sauce
2 tbsp sake or dry white wine
2 tbsp sesame oil
1 tbsp lemon juice

2 tbsp light brown sugar
1 tsp fresh ginger root, grated
1 clove garlic, crushed

TO GARNISH:
1 small carrot
4 scallions

1 Rinse the fish and pat dry on absorbent paper towels. Cut a few slashes into both sides of each fish.

2 Mix together the soy sauce, sake or wine, oil, lemon juice, sugar, ginger, and garlic in a large, shallow dish.

3 Place the fish in the marinade and turn them over so that they are well coated on both sides. Let stand in the refrigerator for 1–6 hours.

4 Meanwhile, prepare the garnish. Using a sharp knife, cut the carrot into even-size thin sticks and clean and shred the scallions.

5 Broil the fish over hot coals for 10 minutes, turning them once.

6 Scatter the chopped scallions and sliced carrot over the fish and then transfer the fish to a warm serving dish. Serve immediately.

VARIATION

Use sole instead of the flounders, and scatter over some toasted sesame seeds instead of the carrot and scallions, if you prefer.

Vegetables, & Rice, Noodles

As vegetables are so plentiful and diverse in the Far East, they play a major role in the diet. Other ingredients, such as bean curd, are added to the vegetarian diet, which is both a healthy and economical choice. Bean curd is produced from the soya bean, which is grown in abundance in these countries. The variety of bean curd is frequently used in stir-frying for texture, and it is perfect for absorbing all of the component flavors of the dish.

The wok is perfect for cooking vegetables as it cooks them very quickly which helps to retain nutrients and crispness, and thus produces a range of colorful and flavorful recipes. Some of the dishes contained in this chapter are ideal accompaniments whilst others, such as vegetable curries, are combined with spices to produce more substantial main meals.

The following chapter shows the wonderful versatility of vegetables and contains something for everyone, which should delight vegetarians and meat-eaters alike.

Stir-Fried Japanese Mushroom Noodles

Serves 4

INGREDIENTS

9 ounces Japanese egg noodles

2 tbsp sunflower oil

1 red onion, sliced

1 clove garlic, crushed

1 pound mixed mushrooms
(shiitake, oyster, brown cap)

12 ounces bok choy
(or Chinese cabbage)

2 tbsp sweet sherry

6 tbsp soy sauce

4 scallions, sliced

1 tbsp toasted sesame seeds

1 Place the Japanese egg noodles in a large bowl. Pour over enough boiling water to cover, and set aside to soak for 10 minutes.

2 Heat the sunflower oil in a large preheated wok.

3 Add the red onion and garlic to the wok and stir-fry for 2–3 minutes, or until softened.

4 Add the mushrooms to the wok and stir-fry for about 5 minutes, or until the mushrooms have softened.

5 Drain the egg noodles thoroughly.

6 Add the the bok choy (or Chinese cabbage), noodles, sweet sherry, and soy sauce to the wok. Toss all of the ingredients together and stir-fry for 2–3 minutes or until the liquid is just bubbling.

7 Transfer the mushroom noodles to warm serving bowls and scatter with sliced scallions and toasted sesame seeds. Serve the stir-fried noodles immediately.

COOK'S TIP

*The variety of mushrooms
in supermarkets has
greatly improved and a
good mixture should
be easily obtainable.
If not, use the more
common button and
flat mushrooms.*

Stir-Fried Vegetables with Sherry & Soy Sauce

Serves 4

INGREDIENTS

2 tbsp sunflower oil

1 red onion, sliced

3–4 medium carrots, thinly sliced

6 ounces zucchini, sliced diagonally

1 red bell pepper, seeded and sliced

1 small head Chinese cabbage, shredded

¾ cup bean sprouts

8 ounce can bamboo shoots, drained

1¼ cup cashew nuts, toasted

SAUCE:

3 tbsp medium sherry

3 tbsp light soy sauce

1 tsp ground ginger

1 clove garlic, crushed

1 tsp cornstarch

1 tbsp tomato paste

1 Heat the sunflower oil in a large preheated wok.

2 Add the red onion slices to the wok and stir-fry for 2–3 minutes, or until just beginning to soften.

3 Add the carrots, zucchini, and bell pepper slices to the wok and stir-fry for a further 5 minutes.

4 Add the Chinese cabbage, bean sprouts, and bamboo shoots to the wok and heat through for 2–3 minutes, or until the leaves just begin to wilt.

5 Scatter the cashew nuts over the top of the vegetables.

6 Mix together the sherry, soy sauce, ginger, garlic, cornstarch, and tomato paste.

7 Pour the mixture over the vegetables and toss well. Simmer gently for 2–3 minutes, or until the juices start to thicken. Serve immediately.

COOK'S TIP

Use any mixture of fresh vegetables that you have to hand in this very versatile dish.

Stir-Fried Bok Choy with Red Onion & Cashew Nuts

Serves 4

INGREDIENTS

2 tbsp peanut oil
2 red onions, cut into thin wedges

6 ounces red cabbage, thinly
shredded

8 ounces bok choy
2 tbsp plum sauce
1 cup roasted cashew nuts

1 Heat the peanut oil in a large preheated wok.

2 Add the onion wedges to the wok and stir-fry for about 5 minutes, or until the onions are just beginning to brown.

3 Add the red cabbage to the wok and stir-fry for a further 2–3 minutes.

4 Add the bok choy to the wok and stir-fry for about 5 minutes, or until the leaves have wilted.

5 Drizzle the plum sauce over the vegetables,

toss together until well combined, and heat until the liquid is bubbling.

6 Scatter with the roasted cashew nuts and transfer to warm serving bowls. Serve immediately.

COOK'S TIP

Plum sauce has a unique, fruity flavor– a sweet and sour with a difference.

VARIATION

Use unsalted peanuts instead of the cashew nuts, if desired.

Bean Curd with Soy Sauce, Green Bell Peppers, & Crispy Onions

Serves 4

INGREDIENTS

12 ounces bean curd	1 tbsp sweet chili sauce	1 green bell pepper, seeded and
2 cloves garlic, crushed	6 tbsp sunflower oil	diced
4 tbsp soy sauce	1 onion, sliced	1 tbsp sesame oil

1 Drain the bean curd and, using a sharp knife, cut it into bite-size pieces. Place the bean curd pieces in a shallow nonmetallic dish.

2 Mix together the garlic, soy sauce, and sweet chili sauce and drizzle over the bean curd. Toss well to coat each piece and set aside to marinate for about 20 minutes.

3 Meanwhile, heat the sunflower oil in a large preheated wok.

4 Add the onion slices to the wok and stir-fry over a high heat until they brown and become crispy. Remove the onion slices with a slotted spoon and drain on absorbent kitchen paper.

5 Add the bean curd to the hot oil and stir-fry for about 5 minutes.

6 Remove all but 1 tablespoon of the oil from the wok. Add the bell pepper to the wok and stir-fry for 2–3 minutes, or until it has softened.

7 Return the bean curd and onions to the wok and heat through, stirring occasionally. Drizzle with the sesame oil.

8 Transfer to serving plates and serve immediately.

COOK'S TIP

If you are in a real hurry, buy ready-marinated bean curd from your supermarket.

Stir-Fried Green Beans with Lettuce & Black Bean Sauce

Serves 4

INGREDIENTS

1 tsp chili oil

2 tbsp butter

1½ cups fine green beans, sliced

4 shallots, sliced

1 clove garlic, crushed

3½ ounces shiitake mushrooms, thinly sliced

1 iceberg lettuce, shredded

4 tbsp black bean sauce

1 Heat the chili oil and butter in a large preheated wok.

2 Add the green beans, shallots, garlic, and mushrooms to the wok and stir-fry for 2–3 minutes.

3 Add the shredded lettuce to the wok and stir-fry until the leaves have wilted.

4 Stir the black bean sauce into the mixture in the wok and heat through, tossing to mix, until the sauce is bubbling. Serve.

COOK'S TIP

To make your own black bean sauce, soak ⅓ cup dried black beans overnight in cold water. Drain and place in a pan of cold water, boil for 10 minutes, then drain. Return the beans to the pan with 2 cups vegetable stock and boil. Blend 1 tablespoon each of malt vinegar, soy sauce, sugar, 1½ teaspoons cornstarch, 1 chopped red chili, and ½ inch ginger root. Add to the pan and simmer for 40 minutes.

COOK'S TIP

If possible, use Chinese green beans, which are tender and can be eaten whole. They are available from specialty Chinese stores.

Deep-Fried Zucchini

Serves 4

INGREDIENTS

1 pound zucchini

1 egg white

⅓ cup cornstarch

1 tsp salt

1 tsp Chinese five-spice powder

oil, for deep-frying

1 Using a sharp knife, slice the zucchini into rings or sticks.

2 Place the egg white in a small mixing bowl. Lightly beat the egg white until foamy, using a fork.

3 Mix the cornstarch, salt and five-spice powder and sprinkle onto a large plate.

4 Heat the oil for deep-frying in a large preheated wok.

5 Dip each piece of zucchini into the beaten egg white then coat in the cornstarch mixture.

6 Deep-fry the zucchini, in batches, for about 5 minutes or until pale golden and crispy. Repeat with the remaining zucchini slices or sticks.

7 Remove the zucchini with a slotted spoon and drain on absorbent kitchen paper while you deep-fry the remainder.

8 Transfer the zucchini to warm serving plates and serve immediately.

VARIATION

Alter the seasoning by using chili powder or curry powder instead of the Chinese five-spice powder, if desired.

Deep-Fried Chili Corn Balls

Serves 4

INGREDIENTS

6 scallions, sliced

3 tbsp fresh cilantro, chopped

8 ounces canned corn

1 tsp mild chili powder

1 tbsp sweet chili sauce

1/4 cup shredded coconut

1 egg

1/3 cup cornmeal

oil, for deep-frying

extra sweet chili sauce, to serve

1 In a large mixing bowl, mix together the scallions, cilantro, corn, chili powder, chili sauce, coconut, egg, and cornmeal. Cover and let stand for about 10 minutes.

2 Heat the oil for deep-frying in a large preheated wok.

3 Carefully drop spoonfuls of the chili and cornmeal mixture into the hot oil. Deep-fry the chili corn balls, in batches, for 4–5 minutes or until crispy and a deep golden brown color.

4 Remove the chili corn balls with a slotted spoon, transfer to paper towels and let drain thoroughly.

5 Transfer to serving plates and serve with an extra sweet chili sauce for dipping.

COOK'S TIP

Cornmeal is a type of meal ground from corn or maize. It is available in most large supermarkets or in healthfood shops.

COOK'S TIP

For safe deep-frying in a round-bottomed wok, place it on a wok rack so that it rests securely. Only half-fill the wok with oil. Never leave the wok unattended over a high heat.

Aspagarus & Red Bell Pepper Packets

Serves 4

INGREDIENTS

3¹/₂ ounces fine tip asparagus	¹/₄ cup bean sprouts	1 egg yolk, beaten
1 red bell pepper, seeded and thinly sliced	2 tbsp plum sauce	oil, for deep-frying
	8 sheets filo pastry	

1 Place the asparagus, bell pepper, and bean sprouts in a large mixing bowl.

2 Add the plum sauce to the vegetables and mix until well combined.

3 Spread out the sheets of filo pastry on a clean counter or chopping board.

4 Place a little of the asparagus and red bell pepper filling at the top end of each filo pastry sheet. Brush the edges of the filo pastry with a little of the beaten egg yolk.

5 Roll up the filo pastry, tucking in the ends and enclosing the filling like a spring roll.

6 Heat the oil for deep-frying in a large preheated wok.

7 Carefully cook the packets, 2 at a time, in the hot oil for 4–5 minutes, or until crispy.

8 Remove the packets with a slotted spoon and drain on absorbent paper towels.

9 Transfer the packets to individual warm serving plates and serve immediately.

COOK'S TIP

Be sure to use fine-tipped asparagus, as it is more tender than the larger stems.

Carrot & Orange Stir-Fry

Serves 4

INGREDIENTS

2 tbsp sunflower oil	2 oranges, peeled and segmented	2 tbsp light soy sauce
1 pound carrots, grated	2 tbsp tomato ketchup	1 cup chopped peanuts
8 ounces leeks, shredded	1 tbsp sugar	

1 Heat the sunflower oil in a large preheated wok.

2 Add the grated carrot and leeks to the wok and stir-fry for 2–3 minutes, or until the vegetables have just softened.

3 Add the orange segments to the wok and heat through gently, ensuring that you do not break up the orange segments as you stir the mixture.

4 Mix the tomato ketchup, sugar and soy sauce together in a small bowl.

5 Add the tomato and sugar mixture to the wok and stir-fry for a further 2 minutes.

6 Transfer the stir-fry to warm serving bowls and scatter with the chopped peanuts. Serve immediately.

VARIATION

Scatter with toasted sesame seeds instead of the peanuts, if wished.

VARIATION

You could use pineapple instead of orange, if wished. If using canned pineapple, make sure that it is in natural juice not syrup, as it will spoil the fresh taste of this dish.

Spinach Stir-Fry with Shiitake & Honey

Serves 4

INGREDIENTS

3 tbsp peanut oil	2 cloves garlic, crushed	2 tbsp clear honey
12 ounces shiitake mushrooms,	12 ounces baby leaf spinach	4 scallions, sliced
sliced	2 tbsp dry sherry	

1 Heat the peanut oil in a large preheated wok.

2 Add the shiitake mushrooms to the wok and stir-fry for about 5 minutes, or until the mushrooms have softened.

3 Add the crushed garlic and baby leaf spinach to the mushrooms in the wok and stir-fry for a further 2–3 minutes, or until the spinach leaves have just begun to wilt.

4 Mix together the dry sherry and clear honey in a small bowl until well combined.

5 Drizzle the sherry and honey mixture over the spinach and heat through.

6 Transfer the stir-fry to warm serving dishes and scatter with scallion slices. Serve immediately, while hot.

COOK'S TIP

Nutmeg complements the flavor of spinach and it is a classic combination. Add a pinch of nutmeg to the dish in step 3, if you wish.

COOK'S TIP

A good quality, dry pale sherry should be used in this recipe. Cream or sweet sherry should not be substituted. Rice wine is often used in Chinese cooking, but sherry can be used instead.

Chinese Vegetable Rice

Serves 4

INGREDIENTS

1¾ cups long grain white rice
1 tsp ground turmeric
2 tbsp sunflower oil
8 ounces zucchini, sliced
1 red bell pepper, seeded and sliced

1 green bell pepper, seeded
  and sliced
1 green chili, seeded and
  finely chopped
1 medium carrot, coarsely grated

¾ cup bean sprouts
6 scallions, sliced, plus extra to
  garnish
2 tbsp soy sauce
salt

1 Place the rice and ground turmeric in a large saucepan of lightly salted water and bring to a boil. Reduce the heat and simmer until the rice is just tender. Drain the rice thoroughly and press out any excess water with a sheet of double thickness paper towels.

2 Heat the sunflower oil in a large preheated wok.

3 Add the zucchini to the wok and stir-fry for about 2 minutes.

4 Add the bell peppers and chili to the wok and stir-fry for 2–3 minutes.

5 Add the cooked rice to the mixture in the wok, a little at a time, tossing well after each addition.

6 Add the carrots, bean sprouts, and scallions to the wok and stir-fry for a further 2 minutes. Drizzle the Chinese vegetable rice with soy sauce and serve at once, garnished with extra scallions, if desired.

VARIATION

For real luxury, add a few saffron strands infused in boiling water instead of the turmeric.

Sweet & Sour Cauliflower & Cilantro Stir-Fry

Serves 4

INGREDIENTS

1 pound cauliflower florets	3½ ounces snow peas	3 tbsp fresh lime juice
2 tbsp sunflower oil	1 ripe mango, sliced	1 tbsp clear honey
1 onion, sliced	½ cup bean sprouts	6 tbsp coconut milk
3–4 medium carrots, sliced	3 tbsp chopped fresh cilantro	salt

1 Bring a large saucepan of lightly salted water to a boil. Lower the heat slightly, add the cauliflower flowerets to the pan and cook for about 2 minutes. Remove from the heat and drain the cauliflower thoroughly in a colander.

2 Heat the sunflower oil in a large preheated wok.

3 Add the onion and carrots to the wok and stir-fry for about 5 minutes.

4 Add the drained cauliflower and snow peas to the wok and stir-fry for 2–3 minutes.

5 Add the mango and bean sprouts to the wok and stir-fry for about 2 minutes.

6 Mix together the cilantro, lime juice, honey, and coconut milk in a bowl.

7 Add the cilantro mixture and stir-fry for

VARIATION

Use broccoli instead of the cauliflower as an alternative, if wished.

about 2 minutes or until the juices are bubbling.

8 Transfer the stir-fry to serving dishes and serve immediately.

Broccoli & Chinese Cabbage with Black Bean Sauce

Serves 4

INGREDIENTS

1 pound broccoli florets
2 tbsp sunflower oil
1 onion, sliced

2 cloves garlic, thinly sliced
¼ cup slivered almonds

1 head Chinese cabbage, shredded
4 tbsp black bean sauce

1 Bring a large saucepan of water to a boil. Add the broccoli florets to the pan and cook for 1 minute. Drain the broccoli thoroughly.

2 Meanwhile, heat the sunflower oil in a large preheated wok.

3 Add the onion and garlic to the wok and stir-fry until just beginning to brown.

4 Add the drained broccoli florets and the flaked almonds to the mixture in the wok and stir-fry for a further 2–3 minutes.

5 Add the Chinese cabbage to the wok and stir-fry for a further 2 minutes.

6 Stir the black bean sauce into the vegetables in the wok, tossing to mix, and cook until the juices are just beginning to bubble.

7 Transfer the vegetables to warm serving bowls and serve immediately.

VARIATION

Use unsalted cashew nuts instead of the almonds, if wished.

Chinese Mushrooms with Deep-Fried Bean Curd

Serves 4

INGREDIENTS

1 ounce dried Chinese mushrooms	4 tbsp cornstarchoil, for deep-frying	1-inch piece of ginger root, grated
1 pound bean curd	2 cloves garlic, finely chopped	1 cup frozen or fresh peas

1 Place the Chinese mushrooms in a large bowl. Pour in enough boiling water to cover and let stand for about 10 minutes.

2 Meanwhile, cut the bean curd into bite-size cubes, using a sharp knife.

3 Place the cornstarch in a medium-size bowl.

4 Toss the bean curd in the cornstarch until thoroughly and evenly coated.

5 Heat the oil for deep-frying in a large preheated wok.

6 Add the cubes of bean curd to the wok and deep-fry, in batches, for 2–3 minutes, or until golden and crispy. Remove the bean curd with a slotted spoon and let drain on absorbent paper towels.

7 Drain off all but 2 tablespoons of oil from the wok. Add the garlic, ginger, and Chinese mushrooms to the wok and stir-fry for 2–3 minutes.

8 Return the cooked bean curd to the wok and add the peas. Heat through for 1 minute, then serve hot.

COOK'S TIP

Use marinated bean curd for extra flavor.

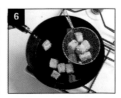

Stir-Fried Butternut Squash with Cashew Nuts & Cilantro

Serves 4

INGREDIENTS

2¼ pounds butternut squash, peeled	1 tsp cumin seeds	TO GARNISH:
3 tbsp peanut oil	2 tbsp chopped cilantro	freshly grated lime zest
1 onion, sliced	⅔ cup coconut milk	fresh cilantro
2 cloves garlic, crushed	½ cup water	lime wedges
1 tsp coriander seeds	1 cup salted cashew nuts	

1 Using a sharp knife, slice the butternut squash into small, bite-size cubes.

2 Heat the peanut oil in a large preheated wok.

3 Add the squash, onion, and garlic to the wok and stir-fry for 5 minutes.

4 Stir in the coriander seeds, cumin, and fresh cilantro and stir-fry for 1 minute.

5 Add the coconut milk and water to the wok and bring to a boil. Cover the wok and simmer for 10–15 minutes, or until the squash is tender.

6 Add the cashew nuts and stir to combine.

7 Transfer to warm serving dishes and garnish with freshly grated lime zest, fresh cilantro, and wedges of lime Serve hot.

COOK'S TIP

If you do not have coconut milk, grate some creamed coconut into the dish with the water in step 5.

Quorn with Ginger & Mixed Vegetables

Serves 4

INGREDIENTS

1 tbsp grated fresh ginger root	1 clove garlic, crushed	3–4 medium carrots, sliced
1 tsp ground ginger	2 tbsp soy sauce	3/4 cup green beans, sliced
1 tbsp tomato paste	12 ounces Quorn or	4 stalks celery, sliced
2 tbsp sunflower oil	mycoprotein cubes	1 red bell pepper, seeded and sliced
		boiled rice, to serve

1 Place the grated fresh ginger, ground ginger, tomato paste, 1 tablespoon of the sunflower oil, garlic, soy sauce, and Quorn or mycoprotein in a large bowl. Mix well to combine, stirring carefully so that you don't break up the Quorn or mycoprotein. Cover and marinate for 20 minutes.

2 Heat the remaining sunflower oil in a large preheated wok.

3 Add the marinated Quorn mixture to the wok and stir-fry for about 2 minutes.

4 Add the carrots, green beans, celery, and red bell pepper to the wok and stir-fry for a further 5 minutes.

5 Transfer the stir-fry to warm serving dishes and serve immediately with freshly cooked boiled rice.

VARIATION

Use bean curd instead of the Quorn, if you prefer.

COOK'S TIP

Ginger root will keep for several weeks in a cool, dry place. Ginger root can also be kept frozen – break off lumps as needed.

Leeks with Baby Corn Cobs & Yellow Bean Sauce

Serves 4

INGREDIENTS
---

3 tbsp peanut oil	8 ounces Chinese cabbage, shredded	6 scallions, sliced
1 pound leeks, sliced	6 ounces baby corn cobs, halved	4 tbsp yellow bean sauce

---

1 Heat the peanut oil in a large preheated wok.

2 Add the leeks, shredded Chinese cabbage, and baby corn cobs to the wok and stir-fry over a high heat for about 5 minutes, or until the edges of the vegetables are beginning to brown slightly.

3 Add the scallions to the wok, stirring to combine.

4 Add the yellow bean sauce to the mixture in the wok and stir-fry for a further 2 minutes, or until heated through.

5 Transfer to warm serving dishes and serve immediately.

COOK'S TIP

Yellow bean sauce adds an authentic Chinese flavour to stir-fries. It is made from crushed salted soya beans mixed with flour and spices to make a thick paste. It is mild in flavour and is excellent with a range of vegetables.

COOK'S TIP

Baby corn cobs are sweeter and have a more delicate flavor than the larger corn cobs and are therefore perfect for stir-frying.

Vegetable Stir-Fry

Serves 4

INGREDIENTS

3 tbsp olive oil
8 baby onions, halved
1 eggplant, cubed
8 ounces zucchini, sliced

8 ounces open-cap mushrooms, halved
2 cloves garlic, crushed
14 ounce can chopped tomatoes

2 tbsp sun-dried tomato paste
freshly ground black pepper
fresh basil leaves, to garnish

1 Heat the olive oil in a large preheated wok.

2 Add the baby onions and eggplant to the wok and stir-fry for 5 minutes, or until the vegetables are golden and just beginning to soften.

3 Add the zucchini, mushrooms, garlic, tomatoes, and tomato paste to the wok and stir-fry for about 5 minutes. Reduce the heat and simmer for 10 minutes, or until the vegetables are tender.

4 Season with freshly ground black pepper and scatter with fresh basil leaves. Serve immediately.

VARIATION

If you want to serve this as a vegetarian main meal, add cubed bean curd in step 3.

COOK'S TIP

Wok cooking is an excellent means of cooking for vegetarians as it is a quick and easy way of serving up delicious dishes of crisp, tasty vegetables. All ingredients should be cut into uniform sizes with as many cut surfaces e xposed as possible for quick cooking.

Stir-Fried Bell Pepper Trio with Chestnuts & Garlic

Serves 4

INGREDIENTS

8 ounces leeks

oil, for deep-frying

3 tbsp peanut oil

1 yellow bell pepper, seeded and diced

1 green bell pepper, seeded and diced

1 red bell pepper, seeded and diced

7 ounce can water chestnuts, drained and sliced

2 cloves garlic, crushed

3 tbsp light soy sauce

1 To make the garnish, finely slice the leeks into thin strips, using a sharp knife.

2 Heat the oil for deep-frying in a wok and cook the leeks for 2–3 minute, or until crispy. Set the crispy leeks aside until they are required.

3 Heat the 3 tablespoons of peanut oil in the wok.

4 Add the bell peppers to the wok and stir-fry over a high heat for about 5 minutes, or until they are just beginning to brown at the edges and to soften.

5 Add the sliced water chestnuts, garlic, and light soy sauce to the wok and stir-fry all of the vegetables for a further 2–3 minutes.

6 Spoon the bell pepper stir-fry onto warm serving plates.

7 Garnish the stir-fry with the crispy leeks and serve.

VARIATION

Add 1 tbsp of hoisin sauce with the soy sauce in step 5 for extra flavor and spice.

Spiced Eggplant Stir-Fry

Serves 4

INGREDIENTS

3 tbsp peanut oil	2 red chiles, seeded and very	3 tbsp mango chutney
2 onions, sliced	finely chopped	oil, for deep-frying
2 cloves garlic, chopped	2 tbsp sugar	2 cloves garlic, sliced, to garnish
2 eggplants, diced	6 scallions, sliced	

1 Heat the peanut oil in a large preheated wok.

2 Add the onions and chopped garlic to the wok, stirring well.

3 Add the eggplants and chiles to the wok and stir-fry for 5 minutes.

4 Add the sugar, scallions, and mango chutney to the wok, stirring well. Reduce the heat slightly, cover, and simmer, stirring from time to time, for about 15 minutes or until the eggplants are tender.

5 Transfer the stir-fry to warm serving bowls and keep warm. Heat the oil for deep-frying in the wok and quickly stir-fry the slices of garlic. Garnish the bowls of stir-fry with the deep-fried garlic and serve immediately.

COOK'S TIP

Keep the vegetables moving around the wok as the eggplant will soak up the oil very quickly and may begin to burn if left unattended.

COOK'S TIP

The "hotness" of chiles varies enormously, so always use with caution, but as a general guide the smaller they are the hotter they will be. The seeds are the hottest part and so are usually discarded.

Stir-Fried Vegetables with Peanuts & Eggs

Serves 4

INGREDIENTS

2 eggs	1 red bell pepper, seeded and	2 tbsp soy sauce
3–4 medium carrots	thinly sliced	1/3 cup salted peanuts, chopped
12 ounces white cabbage	3/4 cup bean sprouts	
2 tbsp vegetable oil	1 tbsp tomato ketchup	

1 Bring a small saucepan of water to a boil. Add the eggs to the pan and cook for about 7 minutes. Remove the eggs from the pan and cool under cold running water for 1 minute.

2 Carefully peel the shells from the eggs and then cut the eggs into quarters.

3 Peel and coarsely grate the carrots.

4 Using a sharp knife, thinly shred the white cabbage.

5 Heat the vegetable oil in a large preheated wok.

6 Add the carrots, white cabbage, and bell pepper to the wok and stir-fry for 3 minutes.

7 Add the bean sprouts to the wok and stir-fry for 2 minutes.

8 Add the tomato ketchup, soy sauce, and peanuts to the wok and stir-fry for 1 minute.

9 Transfer the stir-fry to warm serving plates and garnish with the hard-cooked) egg quarters. Serve immediately.

COOK'S TIP

The eggs are cooled in cold water immediately after cooking in order to prevent the egg yolk blackening around the edges.

Spicy Eggplants

Serves 4

INGREDIENTS

1 pound eggplants, rinsed	1 onion, halved and sliced	1 tbsp wine vinegar
2 tsp salt	1 fresh red chili, sliced	1 tsp ground Szechuan pepper
3 tbsp vegetable oil	2 tbsp dark soy sauce	1¼ cups vegetable stock
2 garlic cloves, crushed	1 tbsp hoisin sauce	
1-inch piece fresh ginger	½ tsp chili sauce	
root, chopped	1 tbsp dark brown sugar	

1 Cut the eggplants into cubes if you are using the larger variety, or cut the smaller type in half. Place the eggplants in a colander and sprinkle with the salt. Set aside for 30 minutes to let the bitter juices drain. Rinse the eggplants under cold running water and pat dry with absorbent paper towels.

2 Heat the oil in a preheated wok and add the garlic, ginger, onion, and fresh chili. Stir-fry for 30 seconds and add the

eggplants. Continue to cook for 1–2 minutes.

3 Add the soy sauce, hoisin sauce, chili sauce, sugar, wine vinegar, Szechuan pepper, and vegetable stock to the wok, reduce the heat, and simmer, uncovered, for about 10 minutes, or until the eggplants are cooked through and tender. Increase the heat and boil to reduce the sauce until thickened enough to coat the eggplants. Serve the spicy eggplants immediately.

COOK'S TIP

Sprinkling the eggplants with salt and letting them stand removes the bitter juices, which would otherwise taint the flavor of the dish.

Fried Bean Curd & Vegetables

Serves 4

INGREDIENTS

1 pound bean curd
²/₃ cup vegetable oil
1 leek, sliced
4 baby corncobs, halved
    lengthwise
2 ounces snow peas
1 red bell pepper, seeded and diced

2 ounces canned bamboo shoots,
    drained and rinsed
rice or noodles, to serve

SAUCE:
1 tbsp Chinese rice wine or
    dry sherry

4 tbsp oyster sauce
3 tsp light soy sauce
2 tsp superfine sugar
pinch of salt
¹/₄ cup vegetable stock
1 tsp cornstarch
2 tsp water

1 Rinse the bean curd in cold water and pat thoroughly dry with absorbent paper towels. Cut the bean curd into 1-inch cubes.

2 Heat the oil in a preheated wok until almost smoking. Reduce the heat, add the bean curd, and gently stir-fry until golden brown. Remove from the wok with a slotted spoon and drain thoroughly on absorbent paper towels.

3 Pour all but 2 tablespoons of the oil from the wok and return to the heat. Add the leek, corncobs, snow peas, bell pepper, and bamboo shoots and stir-fry for 2–3 minutes.

4 Add the Chinese rice wine or sherry, oyster sauce, soy sauce, sugar, salt, and vegetable stock to the wok and bring to a boil. Blend the cornstarch with the water to form a smooth paste and stir it into the sauce. Bring the sauce to a boil and cook, stirring constantly, until thickened and clear.

5 Stir the bean curd into the mixture in the wok and cook for about 1 minute until completely heated through. Serve with rice or noodles.

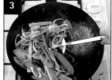

Bean Curd Casserole

Serves 4

INGREDIENTS

1 pound bean curd
2 tbsp peanut oil
8 scallions, cut
  into sticks
2 celery stalks, sliced

4¹/₂ ounces broccoli florets
4¹/₂ ounces zucchini, sliced
2 garlic cloves, thinly sliced
1 pound fresh baby spinach
rice, to serve

SAUCE:
2 cups vegetable stock
2 tbsp light soy sauce
3 tbsp hoisin sauce
¹/₂ tsp chili powder
1 tbsp sesame oil

1 Cut the bean curd into 1-inch cubes and set aside.

2 Heat the oil in a preheated wok. Add the scallions, celery, broccoli, zucchini, garlic, spinach, and bean curd and stir-fry for 3–4 minutes.

3 To make the sauce, mix together the vegetable stock, soy sauce, hoisin sauce, chili powder, and sesame oil in a flameproof casserole and bring to a boil. Add the vegetables and bean curd, reduce the heat, cover, and simmer for 10 minutes. Transfer to a warm serving dish and serve immediately with rice.

COOK'S TIP

This recipe has a green vegetable theme, but alter the color and flavor by adding your favorite vegetables.

VARIATION

Add 3 ounces fresh or canned and drained straw mushrooms with the vegetables in step 2.

Marinated Bean Sprouts & Vegetables

Serves 4

INGREDIENTS

1 pound bean sprouts	2 ounces canned water chestnuts,	1 garlic clove, crushed
2 fresh red chiles	drained and quartered	pinch of Chinese curry powder
1 red bell pepper, seeded and	1 celery stalk, sliced	
thinly sliced	3 tbsp rice wine vinegar	
1 green bell pepper, seeded and	2 tbsp light soy sauce	
thinly sliced	2 tbsp chopped chives	

1 Place the bean sprouts, chiles, bell peppers, water chestnuts, and celery in a large bowl and mix together well.

2 Mix together the rice wine vinegar, soy sauce, chives, garlic, and Chinese curry powder in a bowl and pour the mixture over the prepared vegetables. Toss to mix thoroughly.

3 Cover the salad and chill for at least 3 hours. Drain the vegetables thoroughly, transfer to a serving dish, and serve.

COOK'S TIP

There are hundreds of varieties of chiles and it is not always possible to tell how hot they are going to be. As a general rule, dark green chiles are hotter than light green and red chiles. Thin, pointed chiles are usually hotter than fatter, blunter chiles. However, there are always exceptions and even chiles from the same plant can vary considerably in their degree of spiciness.

COOK'S TIP

This dish is delicious with Chinese roasted meats or served with the marinade and noodles.

Honey-Fried Chinese Cabbage

Serves 4

INGREDIENTS

1 pound Chinese cabbage	1 fresh red chili, sliced	1/2 cup orange juice
1 tbsp peanut oil	1 tbsp Chinese rice wine or dry	1 tbsp sesame oil
1/2-inch piece fresh ginger root,	sherry	2 tsp sesame seeds
grated	4 1/2 tsp light soy sauce	orange zest, to garnish
2 garlic cloves, crushed	1 tbsp clear honey	

1 Separate the Chinese cabbage leaves and shred them finely, using a sharp knife.

2 Heat the peanut oil in a preheated wok. Add the ginger, garlic, and chili to the wok and stir-fry the mixture for about 30 seconds.

3 Add the shredded Chinese cabbage, Chinese rice wine or sherry, soy sauce, honey, and orange juice to the wok. Reduce the heat slightly and simmer for 5 minutes.

4 Add the sesame oil, sprinkle the sesame seeds on top, and mix to combine. Transfer to a warm serving dish, garnish with the orange zest, and serve immediately.

COOK'S TIP

Single-flower honey has a better, more individual flavor than blended honey. Acacia honey is typically Chinese, but you could also try clover, lemon blossom, lime flower, or orange blossom.

VARIATION

Use a western cabbage, such as Savoy, instead of Chinese cabbage if they are unavailable. The flavor will be slightly different and the color darker, but it will still taste just as delicious.

Green Stir-Fry

Serves 4

INGREDIENTS

2 tbsp peanut oil
2 garlic cloves, crushed
$\frac{1}{2}$ tsp ground star anise
1 tsp salt

12 ounces bok choy, shredded
8 ounces fresh baby spinach
1 ounce snow peas
1 celery stalk, sliced

1 green bell pepper, seeded
and sliced
$\frac{1}{4}$ cup vegetable stock
1 tsp sesame oil

1 Heat the peanut oil in a preheated wok.

2 Lower the heat slightly. Add the crushed garlic to the wok and stir-fry for about 30 seconds. Stir in the star anise, salt, bok choy, spinach, snow peas, celery, and green bell pepper and stir-fry for 3–4 minutes.

3 Add the stock, cover, and cook for 3–4 minutes.

4 Remove the lid from the wok and stir in the sesame oil. Mix thoroughly.

5 Transfer the stir-fry to a warm serving dish and serve.

COOK'S TIP

Serve this dish as part of a vegetarian meal or alternatively, with roast meats.

COOK'S TIP

Star anise is an important ingredient in Chinese cuisine. The attractive star-shaped pods are often used whole to add a decorative garnish to dishes. The flavor is similar to licorice but with spicy undertones, and is quite strong. Together with cassia, cloves, fennel seeds, and Szechuan pepper, dried star anise is used to make Chinese five-spice powder.

Crisp Fried Cabbage & Almonds

Serves 4

INGREDIENTS

2 pounds bok choy or collard
   greens
3 cups vegetable oil
³/₄ cup blanched almonds

1 tsp salt
1 tbsp light brown sugar
pinch of ground cinnamon

1 Separate the leaves from the bok choy or collard greens and rinse them well. Pat thoroughly dry with paper towels.

2 Shred the greens into thin strips, using a sharp knife.

3 Heat the vegetable oil in a preheated wok until it is almost smoking.

4 Reduce the heat and add the greens. Cook for about 2–3 minutes, or until the greens begin to float in the oil and have become crisp.

5 Remove the greens from the oil with a slotted spoon and drain thoroughly on absorbent paper towels.

6 Add the almonds to the oil in the wok and cook for 30 seconds. Carefully remove the almonds from the oil with a slotted spoon.

7 Mix the salt, sugar, and cinnamon together and sprinkle onto the greens. Toss the almonds into the greens. Transfer to a warm serving dish and serve the "seaweed" immediately.

COOK'S TIP

Ensure that the greens are completely dry before adding them to the oil, otherwise it will spit. The greens will not become crisp if they are wet when placed in the oil.

Creamy Green Vegetables

Serves 4

INGREDIENTS

1 pound Chinese cabbage, shredded	4 garlic cloves, crushed	4 tsp water
2 tbsp peanut oil	1¼ cups vegetable stock	2 tbsp light cream or
2 leeks, shredded	1 tbsp light soy sauce	unsweetened yogurt
	2 tsp cornstarch	1 tbsp chopped cilantro

1 Blanch the Chinese cabbage in boiling water for 30 seconds. Drain, plunge into cold water or rinse under cold running water, then drain thoroughly again.

2 Heat the oil in a preheated wok and add the Chinese cabbage, leeks, and garlic. Stir-fry for 2–3 minutes.

3 Add the vegetable stock and soy sauce to the wok, reduce the heat to low, cover, and simmer for 10 minutes, or until the vegetables are tender.

4 Remove the vegetables from the wok with a slotted spoon and set aside. Bring the stock to a boil and boil vigorously until reduced by about half.

5 Blend the cornstarch with the water to form a smooth paste and stir the mixture into the stock. Bring to a boil, and cook, stirring constantly, until the stock has thickened and become clear.

6 Reduce the heat and stir in the vegetables and cream or yogurt. Cook over a low heat for 1 minute.

7 Transfer to a serving dish, sprinkle with the chopped cilantro, and serve.

COOK'S TIP

Do not boil the sauce once the cream or yogurt has been added, as it will separate.

Stir-Fried Cucumber with Chilies

Serves 4

INGREDIENTS

2 medium cucumbers	¹/₂-inch fresh ginger root, grated	1 tbsp clear honey
2 tsp salt	2 fresh red chiles, chopped	¹/₂ cup water
1 tbsp vegetable oil	2 scallions, chopped	1 tsp sesame oil
2 garlic cloves, crushed	1 tsp yellow bean sauce	

1 Peel the cucumbers and cut in half lengthwise. Scrape the seeds from the center with a teaspoon and discard.

2 Cut the cucumber into strips and place on a plate. Sprinkle the salt over the cucumber strips and set aside for about 20–25 minutes. Rinse well under cold running water and pat dry with absorbent paper towels.

3 Heat the oil in a preheated wok until it is almost smoking. Lower the heat slightly and add the garlic, ginger, chiles, and scallions and stir-fry for 30 seconds.

4 Add the cucumbers to the wok, together with the yellow bean sauce and honey. Stir-fry for a further 30 seconds.

5 Add the water and cook over a high heat until most of the water has evaporated.

6 Sprinkle the sesame oil over the cucumber and chili stir-fry. Transfer to a warm serving dish and serve immediately.

COOK'S TIP

The cucumber is sprinkled with salt and let stand in order to draw out the excess water, thus preventing a soggy meal!

Spicy Mushrooms

Serves 4

INGREDIENTS

2 tbsp peanut oil

2 garlic cloves, crushed

3 scallions, chopped

10 ounces button mushrooms

2 large open-cap mushrooms, sliced

$4^1/_2$ ounces oyster mushrooms

1 tsp chili sauce

1 tbsp dark soy sauce

1 tbsp hoisin sauce

1 tbsp wine vinegar

$^1/_2$ tsp ground Szechuan pepper

1 tbsp dark brown sugar

1 tsp sesame oil

chopped fresh parsley, to garnish

1 Heat the oil in a preheated wok until almost smoking. Reduce the heat slightly, add the garlic and scallions, and stir-fry for 30 seconds.

2 Add the mushrooms, chili sauce, soy sauce, hoisin sauce, vinegar, pepper, and sugar and stir-fry for 4–5 minutes, or until the mushrooms are cooked.

3 Sprinkle the sesame oil on top. Transfer to a warm serving dish, garnish with parsley, and serve immediately.

COOK'S TIP

This dish is ideal served with rich meat or fish dishes.

COOK'S TIP

Chinese mushrooms are used more for their unusual texture than for their flavor. Tree ears are widely used and are available dried from Chinese grocery stores. They should be rinsed, soaked in warm water for about 20 minutes, and rinsed again before use. Straw mushrooms, so called because they grow on straw, are available, fresh or canned, from Chinese grocery stores and some supermarkets. They have a slippery texture.

Garlic Spinach

Serves 4

INGREDIENTS

2 pounds fresh spinach

2 tbsp peanut oil

2 garlic cloves, crushed

1 tsp chopped lemon grass

pinch of salt

1 tbsp dark soy sauce

2 tsp brown sugar

1 Carefully remove the coarse stems from the spinach. Rinse the spinach leaves in cold water and drain them thoroughly, patting them dry with absorbent paper towels.

2 Heat the oil in a preheated wok until it is almost smoking.

3 Reduce the heat slightly, add the garlic and lemon grass, and stir-fry for 30 seconds.

4 Add the spinach and salt to the wok and stir-fry for 2–3 minutes, or until the spinach has wilted.

5 Stir in the dark soy sauce and brown sugar and cook for a further 3–4 minutes. Transfer to a warm serving dish and serve immediately.

COOK'S TIP

Lemon grass is widely used in Asian cooking. It is available fresh, dried, canned, or bottled. Dried lemon grass must be soaked for 2 hours before using. The stems are hard and are usually used whole and removed from the dish before serving. The roots can be crushed or finely chopped.

COOK'S TIP

Use baby spinach, if possible, as the leaves have a better flavor and look more appealing. If using baby spinach, the stems may be left intact.

Chinese Fried Vegetables

Serves 4

INGREDIENTS

2 tbsp peanut oil
12 ounces broccoli florets
1 tbsp chopped fresh ginger root
2 onions, cut into 8 sections

3 celery stalks, sliced
6 ounces fresh baby spinach
4½ ounces snow peas
6 scallions, quartered
2 garlic cloves, crushed

SAUCE:
2 tbsp light soy sauce
2 tsp superfine sugar
2 tbsp dry sherry
1 tbsp hoisin sauce
⅔ cup vegetable stock

1 Heat the peanut oil in a preheated wok until it is almost smoking.

2 Add the broccoli florets, ginger, onions, and celery and stir-fry for 1 minute.

3 Add the spinach, snow peas, scallions, and garlic and stir-fry for 3–4 minutes.

4 Mix together the soy sauce, sugar, sherry, hoisin sauce, and stock and pour into the wok, mixing well to coat the vegetables. Cover and cook over a medium heat for 2–3 minutes, or until the vegetables are cooked through, but still crisp. Transfer to a warm serving dish and serve immediately.

VARIATION

Any vegetables may be used in this recipe, depending on your preference and its seasonal availability.

COOK'S TIP

You could use this mixture to fill Chinese pancakes. They are available from Chinese grocery stores and can be reheated in a steamer in 2–3 minutes.

Vegetable Chop Suey

Serves 4

INGREDIENTS

1 yellow bell pepper, seeded	1 onion	4$\frac{1}{2}$ ounces bean sprouts
1 red bell pepper, seeded	2 ounces snow peas	2 tsp light brown sugar
1 carrot, peeled	2 tbsp peanut oil	2 tbsp light soy sauce
1 zucchini	3 garlic cloves, crushed	$\frac{1}{2}$ cup vegetable stock
1 fennel bulb	1 tsp grated fresh ginger root	

1 Cut the yellow and red bell peppers, carrot, zucchini, and fennel into very thin slices. Cut the onion into quarters and then cut each quarter in half. Slice the snow peas diagonally to create the maximum surface area.

2 Heat the oil in a preheated wok until it is almost smoking. Lower the heat slightly, add the garlic and ginger, and stir-fry for 30 seconds. Add the onion and stir-fry for a further 30 seconds.

3 Add the bell peppers, carrot, zucchini, fennel, and snow peas to the wok and stir-fry for 2 minutes.

4 Add the bean sprouts to the wok and stir in the sugar, soy sauce, and stock. Reduce the heat to low and simmer for about 1–2 minutes, until the vegetables are tender and coated in the sauce.

5 Transfer the vegetables and sauce to a serving dish and serve immediately.

COOK'S TIP

Use any combination of colorful vegetables that you have on hand to make this versatile dish.

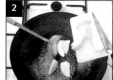

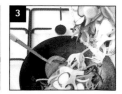

Vegetable Sesame Stir-Fry

Serves 4

INGREDIENTS

2 tbsp vegetable oil

3 garlic cloves, crushed

1 tbsp sesame seeds, plus extra
   to garnish

4 celery stalks, sliced

2 baby corncobs, sliced

2 ounces button mushrooms

1 leek, sliced

1 zucchini, sliced

1 small red bell pepper, seeded
   and sliced

1 fresh green chili, sliced

2 ounces Chinese cabbage,
   shredded

½ tsp Chinese curry powder

2 tbsp light soy sauce

1 tbsp Chinese rice wine or dry
   sherry

1 tsp sesame oil

1 tsp cornstarch

4 tbsp water

1 Heat the oil in a preheated wok until it is almost smoking. Lower the heat slightly, add the garlic and sesame seeds, and stir-fry for 30 seconds.

2 Add the celery, baby corn, mushrooms, leek, zucchini, bell pepper, chili, and Chinese cabbage and stir-fry for 4–5 minutes, until the vegetables are beginning to soften.

3 Mix together the Chinese curry powder, soy sauce, Chinese rice wine or sherry, sesame oil, cornstarch, and water and stir the mixture into the wok. Bring to a boil and cook, stirring constantly, until the sauce thickens and clears. Cook for 1 minute, spoon into a warm serving dish, sprinkle sesame seeds on top, and serve immediately.

COOK'S TIP

The ingredients are fried in vegetable oil in this recipe and not peanut oil, as this would overpower the flavor of the sesame seeds.

VARIATION

You could substitute oyster sauce for the soy sauce, if desired.

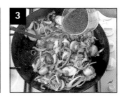

Green Bean Stir-Fry

Serves 4

INGREDIENTS

1 pound thin green beans	$^{1}/_{2}$ tsp ground star anise	2 tsp clear honey
2 fresh red chiles	1 garlic clove, crushed	$^{1}/_{2}$ tsp sesame oil
2 tbsp peanut oil	2 tbsp light soy sauce	

1 Using a sharp knife, cut the green beans in half.

2 Slice the fresh chiles, seeding them first if you prefer a milder dish.

3 Heat the oil in a preheated wok until almost smoking.

4 Lower the heat slightly, add the green beans, and stir-fry for 1 minute.

5 Add the sliced red chiles, star anise, and garlic to the wok and stir-fry for a further 30 seconds.

6 Mix together the soy sauce, honey, and sesame oil and stir into the wok. Cook for 2 minutes, tossing the beans in the sauce to coat. Transfer the beans to a warm serving dish and serve immediately.

COOK'S TIP

This dish makes a great accompaniment to fish or lightly cooked meats with a mild flavor.

VARIATION

This recipe is surprisingly delicious made with Brussels sprouts instead of green beans. Trim the sprouts, then shred them finely. Stir-fry the sprouts in hot oil for 2 minutes, then proceed with the recipe from step 4.

Vegetable Rolls

Serves 4

INGREDIENTS

8 large Chinese cabbage leaves

FILLING:
2 baby corncobs, sliced
1 carrot, peeled and finely
   chopped

1 celery stalk, chopped
4 scallions, chopped
1 ounce canned water chestnuts,
   drained and chopped
2 tbsp unsalted cashews,
   chopped

1 garlic clove, chopped
1 tsp grated fresh ginger root
1 ounce canned bamboo shoots,
   drained, rinsed, and chopped
1 tsp sesame oil
2 tsp soy sauce

1 Place the Chinese cabbage leaves in a large bowl and pour boiling water over them to soften them. Set aside for 1 minute and drain thoroughly.

2 Mix together the baby corncobs, carrot, celery, scallions, water chestnuts, cashews, garlic, ginger, and bamboo shoots in a bowl.

3 Mix together the sesame oil and soy sauce and add to the vegetables, mixing thoroughly.

4 Spread out the Chinese cabbage leaves on a board and spoon an equal quantity of the filling mixture onto each leaf.

5 Roll the leaves up, folding in the sides, to make neat packets. Secure the packets with one or two toothpicks.

6 Place the filled rolls in a small heatproof dish in a steamer, cover, and cook for 15–20 minutes, until the packets are cooked. Serve with a sauce of your choice.

COOK'S TIP

Make the packets in advance, cover, and store in the refrigerator until required, then steam according to the recipe.

Eight Jewel Vegetables

Serves 4

INGREDIENTS

2 tbsp peanut oil

6 scallions, sliced

3 garlic cloves, crushed

1 green bell pepper, seeded and diced

1 red bell pepper, seeded and diced

1 fresh red chili, sliced

2 tbsp chopped water chestnuts

1 zucchini, chopped

4½ ounces oyster mushrooms

3 tbsp black bean sauce

2 tsp Chinese rice wine or dry sherry

4 tbsp dark soy sauce

1 tsp dark brown sugar

2 tbsp water

1 tsp sesame oil

1 Heat the peanut oil in a preheated wok until it is almost smoking.

2 Lower the heat slightly, add the sliced scallions and the garlic, and stir-fry for about 30 seconds.

3 Add the bell peppers, chili, water chestnuts, and zucchini to the wok and stir-fry for 2–3 minutes, or until the vegetables are just beginning to soften.

4 Add the mushrooms, black bean sauce, Chinese rice wine or sherry, soy sauce, sugar, and water to the wok and stir-fry for a further 4 minutes.

5 Sprinkle with sesame oil and serve immediately.

VARIATION

Add 8 ounces diced, marinated bean curd to this recipe for a main course for 4 people.

COOK'S TIP

Eight jewels or treasures form a traditional part of the Chinese New Year celebrations, which start in the last week of the old year. The Kitchen God, an important figure, is sent to give a report to heaven, returning on New Year's Eve in time for the feasting.

Spicy Vegetarian Fried Triangles

Serves 4

INGREDIENTS

1 tbsp sea salt	2 garlic cloves, crushed	vegetable oil, for deep-frying
4½ tsp Chinese five-spice powder	1 tsp grated fresh ginger root	2 leeks, shredded and halved
3 tbsp light brown sugar	2 x 8 ounce cakes bean curd	shredded leek, to garnish

1 Mix the salt, Chinese five-spice powder, sugar, garlic, and ginger in a bowl and transfer to a plate.

2 Cut the bean curd cakes in half diagonally to form two triangles. Cut each triangle in half, and then in half again to form 16 triangles.

3 Roll the bean curd triangles in the spice mixture, turning to coat thoroughly. Set aside for 1 hour.

4 Heat the oil for deep-frying in a wok until it is almost smoking. Reduce the heat slightly, add the bean curd triangles, and fry for 5 minutes, until golden brown. Remove from the wok with a slotted spoon, set aside, and keep warm.

5 Add the leeks to the wok and stir-fry for 1 minute. Remove from the wok with a slotted spoon and drain on absorbent paper towels.

6 Arrange the leeks on a warm serving plate and place the fried bean curd on top. Garnish with the fresh shredded leek and serve immediately.

COOK'S TIP

Fry the bean curd in batches and keep each batch warm until all the bean curd has been fried and is ready to serve.

Chinese Vegetable Casserole

Serves 4

INGREDIENTS

4 tbsp vegetable oil

2 medium carrots, peeled and sliced

1 zucchini, sliced

4 baby corncobs, halved lengthwise

4¹/₂ ounces cauliflower florets

1 leek, sliced

4¹/₂ ounces canned water chestnuts, drained and halved

8 ounces bean curd, diced

1¹/₄ cups vegetable stock

1 tsp salt

2 tsp dark brown sugar

2 tsp dark soy sauce

2 tbsp dry sherry

1 tbsp cornstarch

2 tbsp water

1 tbsp chopped cilantro, to garnish

1 Heat the vegetable oil in a preheated wok until it is almost smoking.

2 Lower the heat slightly, add the carrots, zucchini, corncobs, cauliflower florets, and leek to the wok and stir-fry for 2–3 minutes.

3 Stir in the water chestnuts, bean curd, stock, salt, sugar, soy sauce, and sherry and bring to a boil. Reduce the heat, cover, and simmer for 20 minutes.

4 Blend the cornstarch with the water, mixing to form a smooth paste.

5 Remove the lid from the wok and stir in the cornstarch mixture. Bring the sauce to a boil and cook, stirring constantly, until it has thickened slightly and become clear.

6 Transfer the casserole to a warm serving dish, sprinkle with chopped cilantro, and serve immediately.

COOK'S TIP

If there is too much liquid remaining, boil vigorously for 1 minute before adding the cornstarch to reduce it slightly.

Bamboo Shoots, Ginger, & Bell Peppers

Serves 4

INGREDIENTS

2 tbsp peanut oil

8 ounces canned bamboo shoots, drained and rinsed

1-inch piece fresh ginger root, finely chopped

1 small red bell pepper, seeded and thinly sliced

1 small green bell pepper, seeded and thinly sliced

1 small yellow bell pepper, seeded and thinly sliced

1 leek, sliced

½ cup vegetable stock

1 tbsp light soy sauce

2 tsp light brown sugar

2 tsp Chinese rice wine or dry sherry

1 tsp cornstarch

2 tsp water

1 tsp sesame oil

1 Heat the peanut oil in a preheated wok.

2 Add the bamboo shoots, ginger, bell peppers, and leek to the wok and stir-fry for 2–3 minutes.

3 Stir in the stock, soy sauce, sugar, and Chinese rice wine or sherry and bring to a boil, stirring. Reduce the heat and simmer for 4–5 minutes, or until the vegetables begin to soften.

4 Blend the cornstarch with the water to form a smooth paste.

5 Stir the cornstarch paste into the wok. Bring to a boil and cook, stirring constantly, until the sauce has thickened and become clear.

6 Sprinkle the sesame oil over the vegetables and cook for 1 minute. Transfer to a warm serving dish and serve immediately.

COOK'S TIP

Add a chopped fresh red chili or a few drops of chili sauce for a spicier dish.

Bamboo Shoots with Spinach

Serves 4

INGREDIENTS

3 tbsp peanut oil

8 ounces fresh spinach, chopped

6 ounces canned bamboo shoots,
   drained and rinsed

1 garlic clove, crushed

2 fresh red chiles, sliced

pinch of ground cinnamon

1¼ cups vegetable stock

pinch of sugar

pinch of salt

1 tbsp light soy sauce

1 Heat the peanut oil in a preheated wok.

2 Add the spinach and bamboo shoots to the wok and stir-fry for 1 minute.

3 Add the garlic, chili, and cinnamon to the mixture in the wok and stir-fry for a further 30 seconds.

4 Stir in the vegetable stock, sugar, salt, and soy sauce, cover, and cook over a medium heat for 5 minutes, or until the vegetables are cooked through and the sauce has reduced. Transfer the bamboo shoots and spinach to a warm serving dish and serve.

COOK'S TIP

If there is too much liquid after 5 minutes cooking in step 4, blend a little cornstarch with double the quantity of cold water and stir into the sauce.

COOK'S TIP

Fresh bamboo shoots are rarely available in the West and, in any case, are extremely time-consuming to prepare. Canned bamboo shoots are quite satisfactory, as they are used to provide a crunchy texture, rather than for their flavor.

Sweet & Sour Bean Curd with Vegetables

Serves 4

INGREDIENTS

2 celery stalks	2 garlic cloves, crushed	SAUCE:
1 carrot, peeled	8 baby corncobs	2 tbsp light brown sugar
1 green bell pepper	4½ ounces bean sprouts	2 tbsp wine vinegar
3 ounces snow peas	1 pound bean curd, cubed	1 cup vegetable stock
2 tbsp vegetable oil	rice or noodles, to serve	1 tsp tomato paste
		1 tbsp cornstarch

1 Thinly slice the celery and cut the carrot into thin strips. Seed and dice the bell pepper and cut the snow peas in half diagonally.

2 Heat the vegetable oil in a preheated wok until it is almost smoking. Reduce the heat slightly, add the garlic, celery, carrot, bell pepper, snow peas, and corncobs, and stir-fry for about 3–4 minutes.

3 Add the bean sprouts and bean curd to the wok and cook for 2 minutes, stirring well.

4 Combine the brown sugar, wine vinegar, vegetable stock, tomato paste, and cornstarch, stirring well to mix. Stir into the wok, bring to a boil, and cook, stirring constantly, until the sauce thickens and clears. Continue to cook for

1 minute. Serve with rice or noodles.

COOK'S TIP

Be careful not to break up the bean curd when stirring.

Gingered Broccoli

Serves 4

INGREDIENTS

a2 tbsp peanut oil
1 garlic clove, crushed
2-inch piece fresh ginger root,
    finely chopped
1½ pounds broccoli florets

1 leek, sliced
2¾ ounces canned water
    chestnuts, drained and
    halved
½ tsp superfine sugar

½ cup vegetable stock
1 tsp dark soy sauce
1 tsp cornstarch
2 tsp water

1 Heat the oil in a preheated wok. Add the garlic and ginger and stir-fry for 30 seconds. Add the broccoli, leek, and water chestnuts and stir-fry for a further 3–4 minutes.

2 Add the sugar, stock, and soy sauce, reduce the heat, and simmer for 4–5 minutes, or until the broccoli is almost cooked.

3 Blend the cornstarch with the water to form a smooth paste and stir it into the wok. Bring to a boil and cook, stirring constantly, for 1 minute, until thickened. Transfer to a warm serving dish and serve immediately.

COOK'S TIP

If you prefer a slightly milder ginger flavor, cut the ginger into larger strips, stir-fry as described, and then remove from the wok and discard.

VARIATION

You could substitute water spinach for the broccoli. Trim the woody ends and cut the remainder into 2-inch lengths, keeping the stalks and leaves separate. Add the stalks with the leek in step 1 and add the leafy parts 2 minutes later. Reduce the cooking time in step 2 to 3–4 minutes.

Chinese Potato Sticks

Serves 4

INGREDIENTS

1½ pounds medium-size
  potatoes
8 tbsp vegetable oil
1 fresh red chili, halved

1 small onion, quartered
2 garlic cloves, halved
2 tbsp soy sauce
pinch of salt

1 tsp wine vinegar
1 tbsp coarse sea salt
pinch of chili powder

1 Peel the potatoes and cut into thin slices along their length. Cut the slices into matchsticks.

2 Blanch the potato sticks in boiling water for 2 minutes, drain, rinse under cold water, and drain well again. Pat thoroughly dry with absorbent paper towels.

3 Heat the oil in a preheated wok until it is almost smoking. Add the chili, onion, and garlic and stir-fry for 30 seconds. Remove and discard the chili, onion and garlic.

4 Add the potato sticks to the oil and fry for 3–4 minutes, or until golden.

5 Add the soy sauce, salt, and vinegar to the wok, reduce the heat, and fry for 1 minute, or until the potatoes are crisp.

6 Remove the potatoes with a slotted spoon and drain on absorbent paper towels.

7 Transfer the potato sticks to a serving dish, sprinkle with the sea salt and chili powder, and serve immediately.

VARIATION

Sprinkle other flavorings over the cooked potato sticks, such as curry powder, or serve with a chili dip.

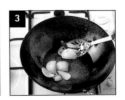

Cucumber & Bean Sprout Salad

Serves 4

INGREDIENTS

12 ounces bean sprouts	2 tomatoes, finely chopped	dash of chili sauce
1 small cucumber	1 celery stalk, cut into	2 tbsp light soy sauce
1 green bell pepper, seeded and	matchsticks	1 tsp wine vinegar
cut into matchsticks		2 tsp sesame oil
1 carrot, peeled and cut into	DRESSING:	16 fresh chives
matchsticks	1 garlic clove, crushed	

1 Blanch the bean sprouts in boiling water for 1 minute. Drain well and rinse under cold water. Drain thoroughly again.

2 Cut the cucumber in half lengthwise. Scoop out the seeds with a teaspoon and discard. Cut the flesh into matchsticks and mix with the bean sprouts, green bell pepper, carrot, tomatoes, and celery.

3 Mix together the garlic, chili sauce, soy sauce, vinegar, and sesame oil. Pour the dressing over the vegetables, tossing well to coat. Spoon onto 4 individual serving plates. Garnish with fresh chives and serve.

COOK'S TIP

The vegetables may be prepared in advance, but do not assemble the dish until just before serving, otherwise the bean sprouts will discolor.

VARIATION

You could substitute 12 ounces cooked, cooled green beans or snow peas for the cucumber. Vary the bean sprouts for a different flavor. Try adzuki bean or alfalfa sprouts, as well as the better-known mung and soy bean sprouts.

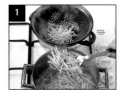

Fried Rice with Spicy Beans

Serves 4

INGREDIENTS

3 tbsp sunflower oil
1 onion, finely chopped
1 cup long grain white rice

1 green bell pepper, seeded and
  diced
1 tsp chili powder

2½ cups boiling water
½ cup canned corn
8 ounces canned red kidney beans
2 tbsp chopped fresh cilantro

1 Heat the sunflower oil in a large preheated wok.

2 Add the finely chopped onion to the wok and stir-fry for about 2 minutes, or until the onion has softened.

3 Add the long grain rice, diced bell pepper, and chili powder to the wok and stir-fry for 1 minute.

4 Pour 2½ cups of boiling water into the wok. Bring to a boil, then reduce the heat, and simmer the mixture for about 15 minutes.

5 Add the corn, kidney beans, and cilantro to the wok and heat through, stirring from time to time.

6 Transfer to a serving bowl and serve hot, scattered with extra cilantro, if wished.

VARIATION

For extra heat, add 1 chopped fresh red chili as well as the chili powder in step 3.

COOK'S TIP

For perfect fried rice, the raw rice should ideally be soaked in a bowl of water for a short time before cooking to remove excess starch. Short grain Asian rice can be substituted for the long grain rice.

Coconut Rice

Serves 4

INGREDIENTS

1¹⁄₃ cups long grain white rice   ½ tsp salt   ¼ cup shredded coconut
2½ cups water   ¹⁄₃ cup coconut milk

1 Rinse the rice thoroughly under cold running water until the water runs clear.

2 Drain the rice thoroughly in a strainer.

3 Place the rice in a wok with 2½ cups water.

4 Add the salt and coconut milk to the wok and bring to a boil. Cover the wok, reduce the heat, and simmer for 10 minutes.

5 Remove the lid from the wok and fluff up the rice with a fork – all of the liquid should be absorbed and the rice grains should be tender.

6 Spoon the coconut rice into a warm serving bowl and scatter with the shredded coconut. Transfer to a serving dish and serve immediately.

COOK'S TIP

The rice is rinsed under cold running water to remove some of the starch and to prevent the grains from sticking together.

COOK'S TIP

Coconut milk is not the liquid found inside coconuts—that is called coconut water. Coconut milk is made from the white coconut flesh soaked in water and milk and then squeezed to extract all of the flavor. You can make your own or buy it in cans.

Stir-Fried Onion Rice with Five-spice Chicken

Serves 4

INGREDIENTS

1 tbsp Chinese five-spice powder

2 tbsp cornstarch

12 ounces boneless, skinless
chicken breasts, cubed

3 tbsp peanut oil

1 onion, diced

1 cup long grain white rice

½ tsp turmeric

2½ cups chicken stock

2 tbsp snipped fresh chives

1 Place the Chinese five-spice powder and cornstarch in a large bowl. Add the chicken pieces and toss to coat all over.

2 Heat 2 tablespoons of the peanut oil in a large preheated wok. Add the chicken pieces to the wok and stir-fry for 5 minutes. Using a slotted spoon, remove the chicken and set aside.

3 Add the remaining peanut oil to the wok. Heat until hot, then reduce the heat.

4 Add the onion to the wok and stir-fry for 1 minute.

5 Add the rice, turmeric, and chicken stock to the wok and bring to a boil.

6 Return the chicken pieces to the wok, reduce the heat, and simmer for 10 minutes, or until the liquid has been absorbed and the rice is tender.

7 Add the chives, stir to mix and serve hot.

COOK'S TIP

Be careful when using turmeric, as it can stain the hands and clothes a distinctive shade of yellow.

Chinese Chicken Rice

Serves 4

INGREDIENTS

1¾ cups long grain white rice
1 tsp turmeric
2 tbsp sunflower oil
12 ounces skinless, boneless
    chicken breasts or thighs,
    sliced

1 red bell pepper, seeded and
    sliced
1 green bell pepper, seeded and
    sliced
1 green chili, seeded and
    finely chopped

1 medium carrot, coarsely grated
¾ cup bean sprouts
6 scallions, sliced, plus extra to
    garnish
2 tbsp soy sauce
salt

1 Place the rice and turmeric in a large saucepan of lightly salted water and cook until the grains of rice are just tender, about 10 minutes. Drain the rice thoroughly and press out any excess water with a double thickness of paper towels.

2 Heat the sunflower oil in a large preheated wok.

3 Add the strips of chicken to the wok and stir-fry over a high heat until the chicken is just beginning to turn a golden color.

4 Add the bell peppers and chili to the wok and stir-fry for 2–3 minutes.

5 Add the rice to the wok, a little at a time, tossing well after each addition, until well combined.

6 Add the carrot, bean sprouts, and scallions to the mixture in the wok and stir-fry for a further 2 minutes.

7 Drizzle with the soy sauce and mix well.

8 Garnish with extra scallions, if wished, and serve at once.

VARIATION

Use pork marinated in hoisin sauce instead of the chicken, if wished.

Sweet Chili Pork Fried Rice

Serves 4

INGREDIENTS

1 pound pork tenderloin

2 tbsp sunflower oil

2 tbsp sweet chili sauce, plus extra
to serve

1 onion, sliced

2–3 medium carrots, cut into
thin sticks

6 ounces zucchini, cut into sticks

1 cup canned bamboo shoots,
drained and rinsed

4³/₄ cups cooked long grain rice

1 egg, beaten

1 tbsp chopped fresh parsley

1 Using a sharp knife, slice the pork thinly.

2 Heat the sunflower oil in a large preheated wok.

3 Add the pork to the wok and stir-fry for 5 minutes.

4 Add the chili sauce to the wok and allow to bubble, stirring, for 2–3 minutes, or until syrupy.

5 Add the onions, carrots, zucchini, and bamboo shoots to the wok and stir-fry for a further 3 minutes.

6 Add the cooked rice and stir-fry for 2–3 minutes, or until the rice is heated through.

7 Drizzle the beaten egg over the top of the fried rice and cook, tossing the ingredients in the wok, until the egg sets.

8 Scatter with chopped fresh parsley and serve immediately, with extra sweet chili sauce, if desired.

COOK'S TIP

For a really quick dish, add frozen mixed vegetables to the rice instead of the freshly prepared vegetables.

Egg Fried Rice with Seven-Spice Beef

Serves 4

INGREDIENTS

1 cup long grain white rice	2 tbsp tomato ketchup	3–4 medium carrots, diced
2¹⁄₂ cups water	1 tbsp Thai seven-spice seasoning	1 cup frozen peas
12 ounces beef fillet	2 tbsp peanut oil	2 eggs, beaten
2 tbsp soy sauce	1 onion, diced	2 tbsp cold water

1 Rinse the rice under cold running water, then drain thoroughly. Place the rice in a saucepan with 2¹⁄₂ cups of water, bring to a boil, cover, and simmer for 12 minutes. Turn the cooked rice out onto a tray and set aside to cool.

2 Using a sharp knife, thinly slice the beef.

3 Mix together the soy sauce, tomato ketchup, and Thai seven-spice seasoning. Spoon this mixture over the beef and toss well to coat evenly.

4 Heat the peanut oil in a large preheated wok.

5 Add the beef to the wok and stir-fry for 3–4 minutes.

6 Add the onion, carrots, and peas to the wok and stir-fry for a further 2–3 minutes.

7 Add the cooked rice to the wok and stir to combine.

8 Lightly beat the eggs with 2 tablespoons of cold water. Drizzle the egg mixture over the rice and stir-fry for 3–4 minutes, or until the rice is heated through and the egg has set.

9 Transfer to a warm serving bowl and serve immediately.

VARIATION

You can use pork tenderloin or chicken instead of the beef, if desired.

418

Stir-Fried Rice with Chinese Sausage

Serves 4

INGREDIENTS

12 ounces Chinese sausage	1–2 medium carrots, cut into	³/4 cup canned pineapple cubes,
2 tbsp sunflower oil	thin sticks	drained
2 tbsp soy sauce	1¼ cups peas	1 egg, beaten
1 onion, sliced	1³/4 cups cooked long grain rice	1 tbsp chopped fresh parsley

1 Using a sharp knife, thinly slice the Chinese sausage.

2 Heat the sunflower oil in a large preheated wok.

3 Add the sausage to the wok and stir-fry for 5 minutes.

4 Stir in the soy sauce and allow to bubble for about 2–3 minutes, or until syrupy.

5 Add the onion, carrots, peas, and pineapple to the wok and stir-fry for a further 3 minutes.

6 Add the cooked rice to the ingredients in the wok and stir-fry for 2–3 minutes, or until the rice is thoroughly heated through.

7 Drizzle the beaten egg over the top of the rice and cook, tossing the ingredients in the wok, until the egg sets.

8 Transfer the stir-fried rice to a large, warm serving bowl and scatter with plenty of chopped fresh parsley. Serve immediately.

COOK'S TIP

Cook extra rice and freeze it in preparation for some of the other rice dishes included in this book, as it saves time and enables a meal to be prepared in minutes.

Chinese Risotto

Serves 4

INGREDIENTS

2 tbsp peanut oil	8 ounces Chinese sausage, sliced	1⅓ cups risotto rice
1 onion, sliced	3–4 medium carrots, diced	1¾ cups vegetable or chicken
2 cloves garlic, crushed	1 green bell pepper, seeded and	stock
1 tsp Chinese five-spice powder	diced	1 tbsp fresh chives, snipped

1 Heat the peanut oil in a large preheated wok.

2 Add the onion, garlic, and Chinese five-spice powder to the wok and stir-fry for 1 minute.

3 Add the Chinese sausage, carrots, and green bell pepper to the wok and stir to combine.

4 Stir in the risotto rice and cook for 1 minute.

5 Gradually add the stock, a little at a time, stirring constantly until the liquid has been completely absorbed and the rice grains are tender.

6 Stir the snipped fresh chives into the wok with the last of the stock.

7 Transfer the Chinese risotto to warm serving bowls and serve immediately.

VARIATION

Use a spicy Portuguese sausage if Chinese sausage is unavailable.

COOK'S TIP

Chinese sausage is highly flavored and is made from chopped pork fat, pork meat, and spices.

Crab Congee

Serves 4

INGREDIENTS

1 cup short grain rice	3½ ounces Chinese sausage,	6 scallions, sliced
6¼ cups fish stock	thinly sliced	2 tbsp chopped cilantro
½ tsp salt	8 ounces white crab meat	

1 Place the short grain rice in a large preheated wok.

2 Add the fish stock to the wok and bring to a boil. Reduce the heat, then simmer gently for 1 hour, stirring the mixture from time to time.

3 Add the salt, Chinese sausage, crab meat, scallions, and cilantro to the mixture in the wok and heat through for about 5 minutes.

4 Add a little more water if the congee 'porridge' is too thick.

5 Transfer the crab congee to warm serving bowls and serve immediately.

COOK'S TIP

Short grain rice absorbs liquid more slowly than long grain rice and therefore gives a different textured dish. A risotto rice, such as arborio, would also be ideal for this recipe.

COOK'S TIP

Always buy the freshest possible crab meat; fresh is best, although frozen or canned will work for this recipe. The delicate, sweet flavor of crab diminishes quickly: this is why many Chinese cooks make a point of buying live crabs. In the West, crabs are almost always sold ready-cooked. The crab should feel heavy for its size, and when it is shaken, there should be no sound of water inside.

Chicken Chow Mein

Serves 4

INGREDIENTS

9 ounces medium egg noodles

2 tbsp sunflower oil

9½ ounces cooked chicken breasts, shredded

1 clove garlic, finely chopped

1 red bell pepper, seeded and thinly sliced

3½ ounces shiitake mushrooms, sliced

6 scallions, sliced

½ cup bean sprouts

3 tbsp soy sauce

1 tbsp sesame oil

1 Place the egg noodles in a large bowl or dish and break them up slightly.

2 Pour enough boiling water over the noodles to cover and let stand while you are preparing the other ingredients.

3 Heat the sunflower oil in a large preheated wok.

4 Add the shredded chicken, finely chopped garlic, bell pepper slices, mushrooms, scallions, and bean sprouts to the wok and stir-fry for about 5 minutes.

5 Drain the noodles thoroughly. Add the noodles to the wok, toss well, and stir-fry for a further 5 minutes.

6 Drizzle the soy sauce and sesame oil over the chow mein and toss until well combined.

7 Transfer the chicken chow mein to warm serving bowls and serve immediately.

VARIATION

You can make the chow mein with a selection of vegetables for a vegetarian dish, if desired.

Egg Noodles with Chicken & Oyster Sauce

Serves 4

INGREDIENTS

9 ounces egg noodles	2 tbsp peanut oil	3 tbsp oyster sauce
1 pound chicken thighs	3½ ounces carrots, sliced	2 eggs
		3 tbsp cold water

1 Place the egg noodles in a large bowl or dish. Pour enough boiling water over the noodles to cover and let stand for 10 minutes.

2 Meanwhile, remove the skin from the chicken thighs. Cut the chicken flesh into small pieces, using a sharp knife.

3 Heat the peanut oil in a large preheated wok.

4 Add the pieces of chicken and the carrot slices to the wok and stir-fry the mixture for about 5 minutes.

5 Drain the noodles thoroughly. Add the noodles to the wok and stir-fry for a further 2–3 minutes, or until the noodles are heated through.

6 Beat together the oyster sauce, eggs and 3 tablespoons of cold water. Drizzle the mixture over the noodles and stir-fry for a further 2–3 minutes, or until the eggs set. Transfer to warm serving bowls and serve hot.

VARIATION

Flavor the eggs with soy sauce or hoisin sauce as an alternative to the oyster sauce, if wished.

Ginger Chili Beef with Crispy Noodles

Serves 4

INGREDIENTS

8 ounces medium egg noodles	1 red chili, seeded and very	2 tbsp lime marmalade
12 ounces beef fillet	finely chopped	2 tbsp soy sauce
2 tbsp sunflower oil	3½ ounces carrots, cut into	oil, for frying
1 tsp ground ginger	thin sticks	
1 clove garlic, crushed	6 scallions, sliced	

1 Place the noodles in a large dish or bowl. Pour over enough boiling water to cover the noodles and let stand for about 10 minutes while you stir-fry the rest of the ingredients.

2 Using a sharp knife, thinly slice the beef.

3 Heat the sunflower oil in a large preheated wok.

4 Add the beef and ginger to the wok and stir-fry for about 5 minutes.

5 Add the garlic, chili, carrots, and scallions to the wok and stir-fry for a further 2–3 minutes.

6 Add the lime marmalade and soy sauce to the wok and allow to bubble for 2 minutes. Remove the chili beef and ginger mixture, set aside, and keep warm.

7 Heat the oil for frying in the wok.

8 Drain the noodles thoroughly and pat dry with absorbent paper towels. Carefully lower the noodles into the hot oil and cook for 2–3 minutes, or until crispy. Drain the noodles on absorbent paper towels.

9 Divide the noodles between 4 serving plates and top with the chili beef and ginger mixture. Serve immediately.

VARIATION

Use pork or chicken instead of the beef, if desired.

Twice-Cooked Lamb with Noodles

Serves 4

INGREDIENTS

9 ounces egg noodles
1 pound lamb loin fillet, thinly
sliced

2 tbsp soy sauce
2 tbsp sunflower oil
2 cloves garlic, crushed

1 tbsp sugar
2 tbsp oyster sauce
6 ounces baby spinach

1 Place the egg noodles in a large bowl and cover with boiling water. Let soak for about 10 minutes.

2 Bring a large saucepan of water to a boil. Add the lamb and cook for 5 minutes. Drain thoroughly.

3 Place the slices of lamb in a bowl and mix with the soy sauce and 1 tablespoon of the sunflower oil.

4 Heat the remaining sunflower oil in a large preheated wok.

5 Add the marinated lamb and garlic to the wok and stir-fry for about 5 minutes, or until just beginning to brown.

6 Add the sugar and oyster sauce to the wok and stir to combine.

7 Drain the noodles thoroughly. Add the noodles to the wok and stir-fry for a further 5 minutes.

8 Add the spinach to the wok and cook for 1 minute, or until the leaves just wilt. Transfer the lamb and noodles to serving bowls and serve hot.

COOK'S TIP

If using dried noodles, follow the instructions on the packet, as they require less soaking.

Singapore-Style Shrimp Noodles

Serves 4

INGREDIENTS

9 ounces thin rice noodles	1 tbsp sugar	1 red bell pepper, seeded and
4 tbsp peanut oil	8 ounces cooked ham,	thinly sliced
2 cloves garlic, crushed	finely shredded	$3^1/_2$ ounces peeled shrimp
2 red chiles, seeded and very	$1^1/_4$ cups canned water chestnuts,	2 large eggs
finely chopped	drained and sliced	4 tbsp coconut milk
1 tsp grated fresh ginger root	$1^1/_4$ cups mushrooms, sliced	$^1/_4$ cup shredded coconut
2 tbsp Madras curry paste	1 cup peas	2 tbsp chopped fresh cilantro
2 tbsp rice wine vinegar		

1 Place the rice noodles in a large bowl, cover with boiling water, and let soak for about 10 minutes. Drain the noodles thoroughly, then toss them with 2 tablespoons of peanut oil.

2 Heat the remaining peanut oil in a large preheated wok. Add the garlic, chiles, ginger, curry paste, wine vinegar, and sugar to the wok and stir-fry for 1 minute.

3 Add the ham, water chestnuts, mushrooms, peas, and red bell pepper to the wok and stir-fry for 5 minutes.

4 Add the noodles and shrimps to the wok and stir-fry for 2 minutes.

5 Beat together the eggs and coconut milk. Drizzle the mixture into the wok and stir-fry until the egg sets.

6 Add the shredded coconut and chopped cilantro to the wok and toss to combine. Transfer the noodles to warm serving dishes and serve immediately.

VARIATION

Egg noodles may be used instead of rice noodles, if desired.

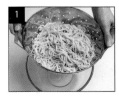

Sweet & Sour Noodles

Serves 4

INGREDIENTS

3 tbsp fish sauce	12 ounces rice noodles, soaked in	8 ounces peeled jumbo shrimp
2 tbsp distilled white vinegar	boiling water for 5 minutes	½ cup chopped peanuts
2 tbsp palm sugar or brown sugar	8 scallions, sliced	1 tsp chili flakes, to garnish
2 tbsp tomato paste	1 cup grated carrot	
2 tbsp sunflower oil	⅔ cup bean sprouts	
3 cloves garlic, crushed	2 eggs, beaten	

1 Mix together the fish sauce, vinegar, sugar, and tomato paste in a small bowl. Set aside until required.

2 Heat the sunflower oil in a large preheated wok.

3 Add the garlic to the wok and stir-fry for 30 seconds.

4 Drain the noodles thoroughly and add them to the wok, together with the fish sauce and tomato paste mixture. Mix well to combine.

5 Add the scallions, carrot, and bean sprouts to the mixture in the wok and stir-fry for 2–3 minutes.

6 Move the contents of the wok to one side, add the beaten eggs to the empty part of the wok, and cook until the egg sets. Add the noodles, shrimp, and peanuts to the wok and toss together until well combined.

7 Transfer to warm serving dishes and garnish with chili flakes. Serve hot.

COOK'S TIP

Chili flakes may be found in the spice section of large supermarkets.

Noodles with Chili & Shrimp

Serves 4

INGREDIENTS

9 ounces thin glass noodles
2 tbsp sunflower oil
1 onion, sliced

2 red chiles, seeded and very
    finely chopped
4 lime leaves, thinly shredded

1 tbsp fresh cilantro
2 tbsp palm or brown sugar
2 tbsp fish sauce
1 pound raw jumbo shrimp, peeled

1 Place the noodles in a large bowl. Pour over enough boiling water to cover the noodles and let stand for 5 minutes. Drain the noodles thoroughly.

2 Heat the sunflower oil in a large preheated wok.

3 Add the onion, chiles, and lime leaves to the wok and stir-fry for 1 minute.

4 Add the cilantro, palm or brown sugar, fish sauce, and jumbo shrimp to the wok and continue stir-frying for about 2 minutes, or until the shrimp turn pink.

5 Add the drained noodles to the wok, toss to mix well, and stir-fry for 1–2 minutes, or until heated through.

6 Transfer to warm serving bowls and serve immediately.

COOK'S TIP

Fish sauce is an essential staple throughout Thailand. You will usually find this labelled as nam pla.

COOK'S TIP

If you cannot buy raw jumbo shrimp, use cooked shrimp instead and cook them with the noodles for 1 minute only, just to heat through.

Stir-Fried Cod & Mango with Noodles

Serves 4

INGREDIENTS

9 ounces egg noodles	1 orange bell pepper, seeded	1 mango, sliced
1 pound skinless cod fillet	and sliced	½ cup bean sprouts
1 tbsp paprika	1 green bell pepper, seeded and	2 tbsp tomato ketchup
2 tbsp sunflower oil	sliced	2 tbsp soy sauce
1 red onion, sliced	1 cup baby corn cobs, halved	2 tbsp medium sherry
		1 tsp cornstarch

1 Place the egg noodles in a large bowl and cover with boiling water. Let stand for about 10 minutes.

2 Rinse the cod fillet and pat dry with absorbent paper towels. Using a sharp knife, cut the cod flesh into thin strips.

3 Place the cod in a large bowl. Add the paprika and toss well to combine.

4 Heat the sunflower oil in a large preheated wok.

5 Add the onion, bell peppers, and baby corn cobs to the wok and stir-fry for about 5 minutes.

6 Add the cod to the wok, together with the mango, and stir-fry for a further 2–3 minutes, or until the fish is tender.

7 Add the bean sprouts to the wok and toss well to combine.

8 Mix together the tomato ketchup, soy sauce, sherry, and cornstarch. Add the mixture to the wok and cook, stirring occasionally, until the juices have thickened slightly.

9 Drain the noodles thoroughly and transfer to serving bowls. Transfer the cod and mango stir-fry to separate serving bowls and serve immediately.

VARIATION

Use other white fish, such as monkfish or haddock, instead of the cod, if desired.

Japanese Noodles with Spicy Vegetables

Serves 4

INGREDIENTS

1 pound fresh Japanese noodles	1 tbsp sunflower oil	12 ounces white cabbage,
1 tbsp sesame oil	1 red onion, sliced	shredded
1 tbsp sesame seeds	3½ ounces snow peas	3 tbsp sweet chili sauce
	1–2 medium carrots, thinly sliced	2 scallions, sliced, to garnish

1 Bring a large saucepan of water to a boil. Add the Japanese noodles to the pan, bring back to a boil, and cook for about 2–3 minutes. Drain the noodles thoroughly.

2 Toss the noodles with the sesame oil and sesame seeds.

3 Heat the sunflower oil in a large preheated wok.

4 Add the onion slices, snow peas, carrot slices, and shredded cabbage to the wok and stir-fry for about 5 minutes.

5 Add the sweet chili sauce to the wok and cook, stirring occasionally, for a further 2 minutes.

6 Add the sesame noodles to the wok, toss well to combine, and heat through for a further 2–3 minutes. (You may wish to serve the noodles separately, so transfer them to serving bowls.)

7 Transfer the Japanese noodles and spicy vegetables to warm serving bowls and garnish with sliced scallions. Serve the noodles immediately.

COOK'S TIP

If fresh Japanese noodles are difficult to get hold of, use dried rice noodles or thin egg noodles instead.

Stir-Fried Rice Noodles with Green Beans & Coconut Sauce

Serves 4

INGREDIENTS

10 ounces rice sticks (wide, flat rice noodles)

3 tbsp peanut oil

2 cloves garlic, crushed

2 shallots, sliced

1½ cups green beans, sliced

3¾ ounces cherry tomatoes, halved

1 tsp chili flakes

4 tbsp crunchy peanut butter

⅔ cup coconut milk

1 tbsp tomato paste

sliced scallions, to garnish

1 Place the rice sticks in a large bowl and pour over enough boiling water to cover. Let stand for 10 minutes.

2 Heat the peanut oil in a large preheated wok.

3 Add the garlic and shallots to the wok and stir-fry for 1 minute.

4 Drain the rice sticks thoroughly.

5 Add the green beans and drained noodles to the wok and stir-fry for 5 minutes.

6 Add the cherry tomatoes to the wok and mix well.

7 Mix together the chili flakes, peanut butter, coconut milk, and tomato paste.

8 Pour the chili mixture over the noodles, toss well to combine, and heat through.

9 Transfer the mixture to warm serving dishes and garnish with scallion slices. Serve immediately.

VARIATION

Add slices of chicken or beef to the recipe and stir-fry with the beans and noodles in step 5 for a more substantial main meal.

Noodle & Mango Salad

Serves 4

INGREDIENTS

9 ounces thread egg noodles

2 tbsp peanut oil

4 shallots, sliced

2 cloves garlic, crushed

1 red chili, seeded and sliced

1 red bell pepper, seeded and
sliced

1 green bell pepper, seeded and
sliced

1 ripe mango, sliced into thin strips

1/4 cup salted peanuts, chopped

4 tbsp peanut butter

1/3 cup coconut milk

1 tbsp tomato paste

1 Place the egg noodles in a large dish or bowl. Pour over enough boiling water to cover the noodles and let stand for 10 minutes.

2 Heat the peanut oil in a large preheated wok.

3 Add the shallots, garlic, chili, and bell pepper slices to the wok and stir-fry for 2–3 minutes.

4 Drain the egg noodles thoroughly.

5 Add the drained noodles and mango slices to the wok and heat through for about 2 minutes.

6 Transfer the noodle and mango salad to warm serving dishes and scatter with chopped peanuts.

7 Mix together the peanut butter, coconut milk, and tomato paste until well combined and then spoon over the noodle salad as a dressing. Serve immediately.

COOK'S TIP

If wished, gently heat the peanut dressing before pouring over the noodle salad.

Egg Fried Rice

Serves 4

INGREDIENTS

²/₃ cup long-grain rice

3 eggs, beaten

2 tbsp vegetable oil

2 garlic cloves, crushed

4 scallions, chopped

1 cup cooked peas

1 tbsp light soy sauce

salt

shredded scallion, to garnish

1 Cook the rice in a saucepan of lightly salted boiling water for 10-12 minutes, until almost cooked, but not soft. Drain well, rinse under cold water, and drain thoroughly again.

2 Place the beaten eggs in a saucepan and cook over a gentle heat, stirring lightly until softly scrambled.

3 Heat the oil in a preheated wok. Reduce the heat slightly, add the garlic, scallions, and peas, and sauté, stirring occasionally, for 1-2 minutes.

4 Stir the rice into the wok, mixing to combine.

5 Add the eggs, soy sauce, and salt to taste and stir to mix the egg in thoroughly.

6 Transfer to a warm serving dish and serve garnished with the shredded scallion.

COOK'S TIP

The rice is rinsed under cold water to wash out the starch and prevent it from sticking together.

VARIATION

You may choose to add shrimp, ham, or chicken, or a combination in step 3.

Fried Rice with Pork

Serves 4

INGREDIENTS

²/₃ cup long-grain rice
3 tbsp peanut oil
1 large onion, cut into 8 sections
8 ounces pork tenderloin,
    thinly sliced

2 open-cap mushrooms, sliced
2 garlic cloves, crushed
1 tbsp light soy sauce
1 tsp light brown sugar

2 tomatoes, peeled, seeded,
    and chopped
¹/₂ cup cooked peas
2 eggs, beaten
salt

1 Cook the rice in a saucepan of lightly salted boiling water for about 15 minutes, until tender, but not soft. Drain well, rinse under cold running water, and drain again thoroughly.

2 Heat the oil in a preheated wok. Add the onion and pork and stir-fry for 3-4 minutes, until just beginning to color.

3 Add the mushrooms and garlic to the wok and stir-fry for 1 minute.

4 Add the soy sauce and sugar to the mixture in the wok and stir-fry for a further 2 minutes.

5 Stir in the rice, tomatoes, and peas, mixing well. Transfer the mixture to a warm dish.

6 Stir the eggs into the wok and cook, stirring, for 2-3 minutes, until beginning to set.

7 Return the rice mixture to the wok and mix well. Transfer to a warm serving dish and serve immediately.

COOK'S TIP

You can cook the rice in advance and chill or freeze it until required.

Vegetable Fried Rice

Serves 4

INGREDIENTS

²/₃ cup long-grain white rice
3 tbsp peanut oil
2 garlic cloves, crushed
¹/₂ tsp Chinese five-spice powder
¹/₃ cup green beans

1 green bell pepper, seeded
and chopped
4 baby corncobs, sliced
1 ounce canned bamboo shoots,
drained, rinsed, and chopped

3 tomatoes, peeled, seeded,
and chopped
¹/₂ cup cooked peas
1 tsp sesame oil
salt

1 Cook the rice in a saucepan of lightly salted boiling water for about 15 minutes. Drain well, rinse under cold running water, and drain thoroughly again.

2 Heat the peanut oil in a preheated wok.

3 Add the garlic and Chinese five-spice powder and stir-fry for 30 seconds.

4 Add the green beans, bell pepper, and corncobs and stir-fry for 2 minutes.

5 Stir the bamboo shoots, tomatoes, peas, and rice into the mixture in the wok and stir-fry for 1 further minute.

6 Sprinkle the vegetable fried rice with sesame oil and transfer to a warm serving dish. Serve immediately.

VARIATION

You could add cashews, dry-fried until lightly browned, in step 5 if desired.

COOK'S TIP

Use a selection of vegetables of your choice in this recipe, cutting them to a similar size in order to ensure that they cook in the same amount of time.

Green Fried Rice

Serves 4

INGREDIENTS

⅔ cup long-grain rice	1 tsp grated fresh ginger root	8 ounces fresh baby spinach
2 tbsp vegetable oil	1 carrot, peeled and cut	2 tsp light soy sauce
2 garlic cloves, crushed	into matchsticks	2 tsp light brown sugar
	1 zucchini, diced	salt

1 Cook the rice in a saucepan of lightly salted boiling water for about 15 minutes. Drain well, rinse under cold water, and drain thoroughly again.

2 Heat 1 tablespoon of the oil in a preheated wok and add the beaten eggs and a further 1 teaspoon of oil. Tilt the wok so that the egg covers the base to make a thin pancake. Cook until lightly browned on the underside, then flip the pancake over and cook on the other side for about 1 minute. Remove from the wok and cool.

3 Heat the oil. Add the garlic and ginger and stir-fry for 30 seconds.

4 Add the scallions, peas, bean sprouts, ham, and shrimp to the wok and stir-fry for about 2 minutes.

5 Stir in the soy sauce and rice and cook for a further 2 minutes. Transfer the rice to a serving dish.

COOK'S TIP

As this recipe contains meat and fish, it is ideal served with simpler vegetable dishes.

VARIATION

Chinese cabbage may be used instead of the spinach, giving a lighter green color to the dish.

Special Fried Rice

Serves 4

INGREDIENTS

²/₃ cup long-grain rice
2 tbsp vegetable oil
2 eggs, beaten
2 garlic cloves, crushed

1 tsp grated fresh ginger root
3 scallions, sliced
³/₄ cup cooked peas
²/₃ cup bean sprouts

1¹/₃ cups shredded ham
5¹/₂ ounces peeled, cooked shrimp
2 tbsp light soy sauce
salt

1 Cook the rice in a saucepan of boiling water for 15 minutes. Drain well, rinse under cold water and drain thoroughly again.

2 Heat 1 tablespoon of the oil in a preheated wok and add the beaten eggs and a further 1 teaspoon of oil. Tilt the wok so that the egg covers the base to make a thin pancake. Cook until lightly browned on the underside, then flip the pancake over and cook on the other side for 1 minute. Remove from the wok and leave to cool.

3 Heat the remaining oil in the wok. Add the garlic and ginger and stir-fry for 30 seconds.

4 Add the spring onions (scallions), peas, beansprouts, ham and prawns (shrimp) and stir-fry for 2 minutes.

5 Stir in the soy sauce and rice and cook for a further 2 minutes. Transfer the rice to serving dishes.

6 Roll up the pancake, slice it very thinly and use to garnish the rice. Serve immediately.

COOK'S TIP

As this recipe contains meat and fish, it is ideal served with simpler vegetable dishes.

Chicken & Rice Casserole

Serves 4

INGREDIENTS

$^2/_3$ cup long-grain rice
2 tsp salt
1 tbsp dry sherry
2 tbsp light soy sauce
2 tbsp dark soy sauce
2 tsp dark brown sugar
1 tsp sesame oil

2 pounds skinless, boneless
 chicken, diced
$3^3/_4$ cups chicken stock
2 open-cap mushrooms, sliced
2 ounces canned water
 chestnuts, drained and
 halved

3 ounces broccoli florets
1 yellow bell pepper, seeded and
 sliced
4 tsp grated fresh ginger root
whole chives, to garnish

1 Cook the rice in a saucepan of boiling water with half the salt for about 15 minutes. Drain well, rinse under cold water, and drain again thoroughly.

2 Place the sherry, soy sauce, sugar, remaining salt, and sesame oil in a large bowl and mix together until well combined.

3 Stir the chicken into the soy mixture, turning to coat well.

Marinate in the refrigerator for about 30 minutes.

4 Bring the stock to a boil in a preheated wok.

5 Add the chicken with the marinade, mushrooms, water chestnuts, broccoli, bell pepper, and ginger.

6 Stir in the rice, reduce the heat, cover, and cook for 25–30 minutes, until the chicken and vegetables are cooked through.

7 Transfer to a serving dish, garnish with chives, and serve.

VARIATION

This dish would work equally well with beef or pork. Chinese dried mushrooms may be used instead of the open-cap mushrooms, if rehydrated before adding to the dish.

Crab Fried Rice

Serves 4

INGREDIENTS

²/₃ cup long-grain rice

2 tbsp peanut oil

4¹/₂ ounces canned white crab meat, drained

1 leek, sliced

²/₃ cup bean sprouts

2 eggs, beaten

1 tbsp light soy sauce

2 tsp lime juice

1 tsp sesame oil

sliced lime, to garnish

1 Cook the rice in a saucepan of boiling salted water for 15 minutes. Drain well, rinse under cold running water, and drain again thoroughly.

2 Heat the peanut oil in a preheated wok.

3 Add the crab meat, leek, and bean sprouts to the wok and stir-fry for 2-3 minutes. Remove the mixture with a slotted spoon and set aside until required.

4 Add the eggs to the wok and cook, stirring occasionally, for 2-3 minutes, until they are just beginning to set.

5 Stir the rice and the crab meat, leek, and bean sprout mixture into the eggs in the wok.

6 Add the soy sauce and lime juice to the mixture in the wok. Cook for 1 minute, stirring to combine, and sprinkle with the sesame oil.

7 Transfer the crab fried rice to a warm serving dish, garnish with the sliced lime, and serve immediately.

VARIATION

Cooked lobster may be used instead of the crab for a really special dish.

Fried Vegetable Noodles

Serves 4

INGREDIENTS

3 cups dried egg noodles
2 tbsp peanut oil
2 garlic cloves, crushed
1/2 tsp ground star anise
1 carrot, peeled and cut into
   matchsticks

1 green bell pepper, seeded and
   cut into matchsticks
1 onion, quartered and sliced
4 1/2 ounces broccoli florets
3 ounces bamboo shoots
1 celery stalk, sliced

1 tbsp light soy sauce
2/3 cup vegetable stock
oil, for deep-frying
1 tsp cornstarch
2 tsp water

1 Cook the noodles in boiling water for 1-2 minutes. Drain well and rinse under cold running water. Leave to drain in a colander.

2 Heat the oil in a preheated wok until smoking. Reduce the heat, add the garlic and star anise, and stir-fry for 30 seconds. Add the remaining vegetables and stir-fry for 1-2 minutes.

3 Add the soy sauce and stock to the wok and cook over a low heat for 5 minutes.

4 Heat the oil for deep-frying until a cube of bread browns in 30 seconds.

5 Form the drained noodles into rounds and deep-fry them in batches until crisp, turning once. Drain thoroughly on paper towels.

6 Blend the cornstarch with the water to form a smooth paste and stir into the wok. Bring to a boil, stirring until the sauce is thickened and clear.

7 Arrange the noodles on a warm serving plate, spoon the vegetables on top, and serve immediately.

COOK'S TIP

Make sure that the noodles are very dry before adding them to the hot oil, otherwise the oil will spit.

Chicken Noodles

Serves 4

INGREDIENTS

8 ounces rice noodles
2 tbsp peanut oil
8 ounces skinless, boneless
    chicken breast, sliced
2 garlic cloves, crushed

1 tsp grated fresh ginger root
1 tsp Chinese curry powder
1 red bell pepper, seeded and
    thinly sliced
3 ounces snow peas, shredded

1 tbsp light soy sauce
2 tsp Chinese rice wine
2 tbsp chicken stock
1 tsp sesame oil
1 tbsp chopped fresh cilantro

1 Soak the rice noodles for 4 minutes in warm water. Drain thoroughly and set aside until required.

2 Heat the oil in a preheated wok. Add the chicken, and stir-fry for 2–3 minutes.

3 Add the garlic, ginger, and curry powder and stir-fry for a further 30 seconds.

4 Add the sliced bell pepper and snow peas and stir-fry for about 2-3 minutes. Then add the drained noodles.

5 Add the soy sauce, Chinese rice wine, and chicken stock to the wok and mix well, stirring occasionally, for 1 minute.

6 Sprinkle the sesame oil and chopped cilantro over the noodles and vegetables.

7 Transfer the noodles and vegetables to a warm serving dish and serve immediately.

VARIATION

You can use pork or duck in this recipe instead of the chicken, if desired.

Curried Shrimp Noodles

Serves 4

INGREDIENTS

8 ounces rice noodles	2 tbsp Chinese curry powder	1 tbsp light soy sauce
4 tbsp vegetable oil	²/₃ cup fish stock	2 tbsp hoisin sauce
1 onion, sliced	8 ounces peeled, raw shrimp	1 tbsp dry sherry
2 ham slices, shredded	2 garlic cloves, crushed	2 tsp lime juice
	6 scallions, chopped	fresh chives, to garnish

1 Cook the rice noodles in a saucepan of boiling water for 3-4 minutes. Drain well, rinse under cold water, and drain thoroughly again. Set aside until required.

2 Heat 2 tablespoons of the oil in a preheated wok.

3 Add the onion and ham and stir-fry for 1 minute.

4 Add the curry powder to the wok and stir-fry for a further 30 seconds.

5 Stir the noodles and stock into the wok and cook for 2-3 minutes. Remove the noodles from the wok and keep warm.

6 Heat the remaining oil in the wok. Add the shrimp, garlic, and scallions and stir-fry for about 1 minute.

7 Add the soy sauce, hoisin sauce, sherry, and lime juice and stir to combine. Pour the mixture over the noodles, toss to mix, and garnish with fresh chives before serving.

VARIATION

You can use cooked shrimp if you prefer, but toss them into the mixture at the last minute—long enough for them to heat right through. Overcooking will result in tough, inedible shrimp.

Singapore Noodles

Serves 4

INGREDIENTS

8 ounces dried egg noodles
6 tbsp vegetable oil
4 eggs, beaten
3 garlic cloves, crushed
1½ tsp chili powder

8 ounces skinless, boneless
    chicken, cut into thin strips
3 celery stalks, sliced
1 green bell pepper, seeded and
    sliced
4 scallions, sliced

1 ounce canned water chestnuts,
    drained and quartered
2 fresh red chiles, sliced
10 ounces peeled, cooked shrimp
6 ounces bean sprouts
2 tsp sesame oil

1 Soak the noodles in boiling water for 4 minutes, or until soft. Drain well on absorbent paper towels.

2 Heat 2 tablespoons of the oil in a preheated wok. Add the eggs and stir until set. Remove the cooked eggs from the wok, set aside, and keep warm.

3 Add the remaining oil to the wok. Add the garlic and chili powder and stir-fry for 30 seconds.

4 Add the chicken and stir-fry for 4-5 minutes, until just beginning to turn golden brown on all sides.

5 Stir in the celery, bell pepper, scallions, water chestnuts, and chiles and cook for a further 8 minutes, or until the chicken is cooked through.

6 Add the shrimp and the reserved noodles to the wok, together with the bean sprouts, and toss to mix well.

7 Break the cooked egg with a fork and sprinkle it over the noodles, together with the sesame oil. Serve immediately.

COOK'S TIP

When mixing precooked ingredients into the dish, such as the egg and noodles, ensure that they are heated right through and are hot when ready to serve.

Spicy Pork & Noodles

Serves 4

INGREDIENTS

12 ounces ground pork
1 tbsp light soy sauce
1 tbsp dry sherry
12 ounces egg noodles
2 tsp sesame oil
2 tbsp vegetable oil

2 garlic cloves, crushed
2 tsp grated fresh ginger root
2 fresh red chiles, sliced
1 red bell pepper, seeded and
    finely sliced

$\frac{1}{4}$ cup unsalted peanuts
3 tbsp peanut butter
3 tbsp dark soy sauce
dash of chili oil
$1\frac{1}{4}$ cups pork stock

1 Mix together the pork, light soy sauce, and dry sherry in a large bowl. Cover and marinate for 30 minutes.

2 Meanwhile, cook the noodles in a saucepan of boiling water for 4 minutes. Drain well, rinse in cold water, and drain again.

3 Toss the noodles in the sesame oil.

4 Heat the vegetable oil in a preheated wok.

Add the garlic, ginger, chiles, and red bell pepper and stir-fry for 30 seconds.

5 Add the pork to the mixture in the wok, together with the marinade. Continue cooking for about 1 minute, until the pork is sealed.

6 Add the peanuts, peanut butter, soy sauce, chili oil, and stock and cook for 2-3 minutes.

7 Toss the noodles in the mixture and serve at once.

VARIATION

Ground chicken or lamb would also be excellent in this recipe instead of the pork.

Chicken on Crispy Noodles

Serves 4

INGREDIENTS

8 ounces skinless, boneless chicken breasts, shredded

1 egg white

5 tsp cornstarch

8 ounces thin egg noodles

$1^2/_3$ cups vegetable oil

$2^1/_2$ cups chicken stock

2 tbsp dry sherry

2 tbsp oyster sauce

1 tbsp light soy sauce

1 tbsp hoisin sauce

1 red bell pepper, seeded and very thinly sliced

2 tbsp water

3 scallions, chopped

1 Mix the chicken, egg white, and 2 teaspoons of the cornstarch in a bowl. Let stand for at least 30 minutes.

2 Blanch the noodles in boiling water for 2 minutes, then drain thoroughly. Heat the oil in a preheated wok. Add the noodles, spreading them to cover the base of the wok. Cook over a low heat for about 5 minutes, until the noodles are browned on the underside. Flip the noodles over and brown on the other side. Remove from the wok when crisp and browned, place on a serving plate, and keep warm. Drain the oil from the wok.

3 Add $1^1/_4$ cups of the chicken stock to the wok. Remove from the heat and add the chicken, stirring well so that it does not stick. Return to the heat and cook for 2 minutes. Drain, discarding the stock.

4 Wipe the wok with paper towels and return to the heat. Add the sherry, oyster sauce, soy sauce, hoisin sauce, red bell pepper, and the remaining chicken stock and bring to a boil. Blend the remaining cornstarch with the water to form a paste and stir it into the mixture.

5 Return the chicken to the wok and cook over a low heat for 2 minutes. Place the chicken on top of the noodles and sprinkle with scallions. Serve immediately.

Cellophane Noodles with Yellow Bean Sauce

Serves 4

INGREDIENTS

6 ounces cellophane noodles
1 tbsp peanut oil
1 leek, sliced
2 garlic cloves, crushed

1 pound ground chicken
1 cup chicken stock
1 tsp chili sauce
2 tbsp yellow bean sauce

4 tbsp light soy sauce
1 tsp sesame oil
chopped chives, to garnish

1 Soak the noodles in boiling water for 15 minutes. Drain the noodles thoroughly and cut them into short lengths with a pair of kitchen scissors. Set aside until they are required.

2 Heat the oil in a preheated wok. Add the leek and garlic and stir-fry for 30 seconds.

3 Add the chicken to the wok and stir-fry for 4-5 minutes, until the chicken is completely cooked through.

4 Add the chicken stock, chili sauce, yellow bean sauce, and soy sauce to the wok and cook for 3-4 minutes.

5 Add the drained noodles and sesame oil to the wok and cook, tossing to mix well, for 4-5 minutes.

6 Spoon the cellophane noodles and yellow bean sauce into a warm serving bowl, sprinkle with chopped chives to garnish, and serve immediately.

COOK'S TIP

Cellophane noodles are available from many supermarkets and all Chinese grocery stores.

Noodles with Shrimp

Serves 4

INGREDIENTS

8 ounces thin egg noodles
2 tbsp peanut oil
1 garlic clove, crushed
1/2 tsp ground star anise

1 bunch scallions, cut into
   2-inch pieces
24 raw jumbo shrimp, peeled
   with tails intact

2 tbsp light soy sauce
2 tsp lime juice
lime wedges, to garnish

1 Blanch the noodles in a saucepan of boiling water for about 2 minutes. Drain well, rinse under cold water, and drain thoroughly again.

2 Heat the oil in a preheated wok until almost smoking.

3 Reduce the heat slightly, add the garlic and star anise to the wok, and stir-fry for about 30 seconds.

4 Add the scallions and shrimp to the wok and stir-fry for 2–3 minutes.

5 Stir in the soy sauce, lime juice, and noodles and mix well. Cook for 1 minute until thoroughly warmed through, then spoon into a warm serving dish, garnish with lime wedges, and serve immediately.

VARIATION

This dish is just as tasty with smaller cooked shrimp, but it is not quite so visually appealing.

COOK'S TIP

Chinese egg noodles are made from wheat or rice flour, water, and egg. Noodles are a symbol of longevity, and so are always served at birthday celebrations—it is regarded as bad luck to cut them.

Beef Chow Mein

Serves 4

INGREDIENTS

1 pound egg noodles

4 tbsp peanut oil

1 pound lean steak, cut into thin strips

2 garlic cloves, crushed

1 tsp grated fresh ginger root

1 green bell pepper, seeded and thinly sliced

1 carrot, peeled and thinly sliced

2 celery stalks, sliced

8 scallions

1 tsp dark brown sugar

1 tbsp dry sherry

2 tbsp dark soy sauce

few drops of chili sauce

1 Cook the noodles in a saucepan of boiling salted water for 4-5 minutes. Drain well, rinse under cold running water, and drain thoroughly again.

2 Toss the noodles in 1 tablespoon of the oil.

3 Heat the remaining oil in a preheated wok. Add the steak and stir-fry for 3-4 minutes, stirring constantly.

4 Add the garlic and ginger and stir-fry for 30 seconds.

5 Add the bell pepper, carrot, celery, and scallions and stir-fry for about 2 minutes.

6 Add the sugar, sherry, soy sauce, and chili sauce and cook, stirring occasionally, for 1 minute.

7 Stir in the noodles, mixing well, and cook for 1–2 minutes, or until completely warmed through.

8 Transfer to a warm serving bowl and serve immediately.

VARIATION

A variety of different vegetables may be used in this recipe for color and flavor—try broccoli, red bell peppers, green beans, or baby corncobs.

Cantonese Fried Noodles

Serves 4

INGREDIENTS

12 ounces egg noodles
1½ pounds lean steak, cut into
    thin strips
3 tbsp vegetable oil

4½ ounces green cabbage,
    shredded
3 ounces bamboo shoots,
    drained
6 scallions, sliced
1 ounce green beans, halved

1 tbsp dark soy sauce
2 tbsp beef stock
1 tbsp dry sherry
1 tbsp light brown sugar
2 tbsp chopped fresh parsley,
    to garnish

1 Cook the noodles in a saucepan of boiling water for 2-3 minutes. Drain well, rinse under cold running water, and drain thoroughly again.

2 Heat 1 tablespoon of the oil in a preheated wok.

3 Add the noodles to the wok and stir-fry for 1-2 minutes. Drain and set aside until required.

4 Heat the remaining oil in the wok. Add the beef and stir-fry for 2-3 minutes.

5 Add the cabbage, bamboo shoots, scallions, and beans to the wok and stir-fry for about 1-2 minutes.

6 Add the soy sauce, stock, sherry, and sugar to the wok, stirring to mix well.

7 Stir the noodles into the mixture in the wok, tossing to mix well.

8 Transfer to serving bowls, garnish with chopped parsley, and serve immediately.

VARIATION

You can use lean pork or chicken instead of the beef in this recipe, if desired— remember to alter the stock accordingly.

Fried Noodles with Mushrooms & Pork

Serves 4

INGREDIENTS

1 pound thin egg noodles	1 onion, cut into 8 sections	2 tbsp light soy sauce
2 tbsp peanut oil	8 ounces oyster mushrooms	1/4 cup pork stock
12 ounces pork tenderloin, sliced	4 tomatoes, peeled, seeded, and	1 tbsp chopped fresh cilantro
2 garlic cloves, crushed	thinly sliced	

1 Cook the noodles in a saucepan of boiling water for 2-3 minutes. Drain well, rinse under cold running water, and drain thoroughly again.

2 Heat 1 tablespoon of the oil in a preheated wok.

3 Add the noodles to the wok and stir-fry for 2 minutes.

4 Using a slotted spoon, remove the noodles from the wok, drain well, and set aside until they are required.

5 Heat the remaining oil in the wok. Add the pork and stir-fry for 4-5 minutes.

6 Stir in the garlic and onion and stir-fry for a further 2-3 minutes.

7 Add the mushrooms, tomatoes, soy sauce, pork stock, and noodles. Stir well and cook for 1-2 minutes.

8 Transfer to a serving dish, sprinkle with chopped cilantro, and serve immediately.

COOK'S TIP

For crisper noodles, add 2 tablespoons of oil to the wok and fry the noodles for 5-6 minutes, turning them once halfway through cooking.

Lamb with Cellophane Noodles

Serves 4

INGREDIENTS

5¹/₂ ounces cellophane noodles

2 tbsp peanut oil

1 pound lean lamb, thinly sliced

2 garlic cloves, crushed

2 leeks, sliced

3 tbsp dark soy sauce

1 cup lamb stock

dash of chili sauce

red chili strips, to garnish

1 Bring a large pan of water to a boil. Add the transparent noodles and cook for 1 minute. Drain the noodles well, rinse under cold running water, and drain thoroughly again.

2 Heat the peanut oil in a preheated wok. Add the lamb to the wok and stir-fry for about 2 minutes.

3 Add the garlic and leeks to the wok and stir-fry for a further 2 minutes.

4 Stir in the soy sauce, stock, and chili sauce and cook for 3-4 minutes, until the meat is cooked through.

5 Add the noodles to the wok and cook for 1 minute, until heated through.

6 Transfer to a serving dish, garnish, and serve.

COOK'S TIP

Chili sauce is a very hot sauce made from chiles, vinegar, sugar, and salt and should be used sparingly. Tabasco sauce can be used as a substitute.

COOK'S TIP

Cellophane noodles are available in Chinese grocery stores. Use egg noodles instead if cellophane noodles are unavailable, and cook them according to package instructions.

Cellophane Noodles with Shrimp

Serves 4

INGREDIENTS

6 ounces cellophane noodles
1 tbsp vegetable oil
1 garlic clove, crushed
2 tsp grated fresh ginger root
24 raw jumbo shrimp, peeled
    and deveined

1 red bell pepper, seeded and
    thinly sliced
1 green bell pepper, seeded and
    thinly sliced
1 onion, chopped
2 tbsp light soy sauce

juice of 1 orange
2 tsp wine vinegar
pinch of brown sugar
$^2/_3$ cup fish stock
1 tbsp cornstarch
2 tsp water
orange slices, to garnish

1 Cook the noodles in a saucepan of boiling water for 1 minute. Drain well, rinse under cold water, and then drain thoroughly again.

2 Heat the oil in a preheated wok. Add the garlic and ginger and stir-fry for 30 seconds.

3 Add the shrimp and stir-fry for 2 minutes. Remove the shrimp with a slotted spoon, set aside, and keep warm.

4 Add the bell peppers and onion to the wok and stir-fry for 2 minutes. Stir in the soy sauce, orange juice, vinegar, sugar, and stock.

5 Return the shrimp to the wok and cook for 8-10 minutes, until cooked through.

6 Blend the cornstarch with the water and add to the wok. Bring to a boil, add the noodles, and cook for 1-2 minutes. Garnish and serve immediately.

VARIATION

Lime or lemon juice and slices may be used instead of the orange. Use 3-5½ tsp of these juices.

Sweets & Desserts

Desserts are almost unheard of in many Oriental
households and the following recipes are either
adaptations of Imperial recipes or use Chinese
cooking methods and ingredients to produce
delicious desserts which would round off
any meal perfectly.

The Chinese do not usually have desserts to finish
off a meal, except at banquets and special occasions.
Sweet dishes are usually served in between main
meals as snacks, but fresh fruit is considered to be
very refreshing at the end of a big meal.

Rice is cooked with fruits, lychees are spiced with
ginger and served with a refreshing orange sorbet,
and wonton wrappers are sealed around a sweet
date filling and laced with honey, to name but a few
of the tempting treats that follow in this chapter.

Sweet Fruit Wontons

Serves 4

INGREDIENTS

12 wonton wrappers
2 tsp cornstarch
6 tsp cold water
oil, for deep-frying

2 tbsp clear honey
selection of fresh fruit (such as kiwi
    fruit, limes, oranges, mango,
    and apples), sliced, to serve

FILLING:
1 cup chopped dried, pitted dates
2 tsp dark brown sugar
1/2 tsp ground cinnamon

1 To make the filling, mix together the dates, sugar, and cinnamon in a bowl.

2 Spread out the wonton wrappers on a chopping board and spoon a little of the filling into the center of each wrapper.

3 Mix together the cornstarch and water and brush this around the edges of the wrappers.

4 Fold the wrappers over the filling, bringing the edges together, then bring the two corners together, sealing with the cornstarch mixture.

5 Heat the oil for deep-frying in a wok until a cube of bread browns in 30 seconds. Fry the wontons, in batches, for 2–3 minutes, until golden. Remove the wontons from the oil with a slotted spoon and drain thoroughly on absorbent paper towels.

6 Place the honey in a bowl and stand it in warm water, to soften it slightly. Meanwhile, arrange the wontons on a serving dish. Drizzle the honey over the wontons and serve immediately with the fresh fruit.

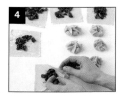

Banana Pastries

Serves 4

INGREDIENTS

DOUGH:
4 cups all-purpose flour
4 tbsp shortening
4 tbsp sweet butter
1/2 cup water

FILLING:
2 large bananas
1/3 cup finely chopped no-need-
　to-soak dried apricots
pinch of nutmeg

dash of orange juice
1 egg yolk, beaten
confectioners' sugar, for dusting
whipped cream or ice cream,
　to serve

1 To make the dough, sift the flour into a large mixing bowl. Add the shortening and butter and rub into the flour with your fingertips until the mixture resembles breadcrumbs. Gradually blend in the water to make a soft dough. Wrap in plastic wrap and chill in the refrigerator for 30 minutes.

2 Mash the bananas in a bowl with a fork and stir in the apricots, nutmeg, and orange juice, mixing well.

3 Roll the dough out on a lightly floured surface and cut out 4-inch rounds.

4 Spoon a little of the banana filling onto one half of each round and fold the dough over the filling to make semicircles. Pinch the edges together and seal by pressing with the prongs of a fork.

5 Arrange the pastries on a nonstick cookie sheet and brush them with the beaten egg yolk to glaze.

6 Cut a small slit in each pastry and cook in a preheated oven at 350°F for about 25 minutes, or until golden brown.

7 Dust with confectioners' sugar and serve with whipped cream or ice cream.

Mango Dumplings

Serves 4

INGREDIENTS

DOUGH:
2 tsp baking powder
1 tbsp superfine sugar
$^2/_3$ cup water
$^2/_3$ cup milk

$3^1/_2$ cups all-purpose flour

FILLING:
1 small mango
4 ounce can litchis, drained

1 tbsp ground almonds
4 tbsp orange juice
ground cinnamon, for dusting

1 To make the dough, place the baking powder and sugar in a large mixing bowl. Mix the water and milk together and then stir this mixture into the baking powder and sugar mixture until well combined. Gradually stir in the flour to make a soft dough. Set the dough aside in a warm place for about 1 hour.

2 To make the filling, peel the mango and cut the flesh from the pit. Roughly chop the mango flesh; reserve half, and set aside for the sauce.

3 Chop the litchis and add to half of the chopped mango, together with the ground almonds. Let stand for 20 minutes.

4 Meanwhile, make the sauce. Blend the reserved mango and the orange juice in a food processor until smooth. Rub the mixture through a strainer to make a smooth sauce.

5 Divide the dough into 16 equal pieces. Roll each piece out on a lightly floured surface into 3-inch rounds.

6 Spoon a little of the mango and litchi filling onto the center of each round and fold the dough over the filling to make semicircles. Pinch the edges together to seal firmly.

7 Place the dumplings on a heatproof plate in a steamer, cover, and steam for about 25 minutes, until cooked through.

8 Remove the dumplings from the steamer, dust with a little ground cinnamon, and serve with the mango sauce.

Sweet Rice

Serves 4

INGREDIENTS

³/₄ cup round grain rice
2 tbsp sweet butter
1 tbsp superfine sugar
8 dried dates, pitted and
   chopped

1 tbsp raisins
5 candied cherries, halved
5 pieces angelica, chopped
5 walnut halves
¹/₂ cup canned chestnut purée

SYRUP:
²/₃ cup water
2 tbsp orange juice
4¹/₂ tsp light brown sugar
1¹/₂ tsp cornstarch
1 tbsp cold water

1 Put the rice in a pan, cover with cold water, and bring to a boil. Reduce the heat, cover, and simmer for 15 minutes, or until the water has been absorbed. Stir in the butter and sugar.

2 Grease a 2¹/₂-cup heatproof bowl. Cover the base and sides with a thin layer of the rice, pressing it in firmly with the back of a spoon.

3 Mix the fruit and walnuts and press them into the rice.

4 Spread a thicker layer of rice on top and then fill the center with the chestnut purée. Cover with the remaining rice, pressing the top down to seal in the purée.

5 Cover the bowl with pleated wax paper and foil and secure with string tied around the rim. Place in a steamer, or stand the bowl in a pan and fill with hot water until it reaches halfway up the sides of the bowl. Cover and steam for 45 minutes. Let stand for 10 minutes.

6 Before serving, gently heat the water and orange juice. Add the sugar and stir to dissolve. Bring the syrup to a boil.

7 Mix the cornstarch with the cold water to form a smooth paste, then stir into the boiling syrup. Cook for 1 minute until thickened and clear.

8 Turn the pudding out onto a serving plate. Pour the syrup over the top, cut into slices, and serve immediately.

Honeyed Rice Puddings

Serves 4

INGREDIENTS

1½ cups round grain rice
2 tbsp clear honey, plus extra
   for drizzling
large pinch of ground cinnamon

3 pieces preserved ginger,
   drained and chopped
15 no-need-to-soak dried
   apricots, chopped

8 whole no-need-to-soak dried
   apricots, to decorate

1 Put the rice in a saucepan and just cover with cold water. Bring to a boil, reduce the heat, cover, and cook for 15 minutes, or until the water has been absorbed.

2 Stir the honey and cinnamon into the rice.

3 Grease 4 × ⅔-cup ramekin dishes or heatproof cups.

4 Blend the apricots and ginger in a food processor to make a paste. Divide the paste into 4 equal portions and shape each into a flat round to fit into the base of the cups.

5 Divide half the rice between the ramekins or cups and place the apricot paste on top.

6 Cover the apricot paste with the remaining rice. Cover the ramekins or cups with wax paper and foil and steam for 30 minutes, or until set.

7 Remove the ramekins or cups from the steamer and let stand for 5 minutes.

8 Turn the desserts out onto warm serving plates and drizzle with clear honey. Decorate with dried apricots and serve.

COOK'S TIP

The desserts may be left to chill in their ramekin dishes or cups in the refrigerator, then turned out and served with ice cream or cream.

Mango Mousse

Serves 4

INGREDIENTS

14 ounce can mangoes in syrup
2 pieces preserved ginger,
    drained and chopped
1 cup heavy cream

4 tsp powdered gelatin
2 tbsp water
2 egg whites
1½ tbsp light brown sugar

preserved ginger and lime zest,
to decorate

1 Drain the mangoes, reserving the syrup. Blend the mango pieces and ginger in a food processor or blender for about 30 seconds, or until smooth.

2 Measure the purée and make up to 1¼ cups with the reserved mango syrup.

3 In a separate bowl, whip the cream until it forms soft peaks. Fold the mango mixture into the cream until combined.

4 Dissolve the gelatin in the water and let cool slightly. Pour the gelatin into the mango mixture in a steady stream, stirring constantly. Let cool in the refrigerator for about 30 minutes, until almost set.

5 Beat the egg whites in a clean bowl until they form soft peaks, then beat in the sugar. Gently fold the egg whites into the mango mixture with a metal spoon.

6 Spoon the mousse into individual serving dishes or tall glasses and decorate with preserved ginger and lime zest. Serve immediately.

COOK'S TIP

The gelatin must be stirred into the mango mixture in a gentle, steady stream to prevent it from setting in lumps when it comes into contact with the cold mixture.

Deep-Fried Bananas

Serves 4

INGREDIENTS

8 medium bananas
2 tsp lemon juice
²/₃ cup self-rising flour

²/₃ cup rice flour
1 tbsp cornstarch
½ tsp ground cinnamon

1 cup water
4 tbsp light brown sugar
oil, for deep-frying

1 Cut the bananas into chunks and place them in a large mixing bowl.

2 Sprinkle the lemon juice over the bananas to prevent discoloration.

3 Sift the self-rising flour, rice flour, cornstarch, and cinnamon into a mixing bowl. Gradually stir in the water to make a thin batter.

4 Heat the oil in a preheated wok until almost smoking, then reduce the heat slightly.

5 Place a piece of banana on the end of a fork and carefully dip it into the batter, draining off any excess. Repeat with the remaining banana pieces.

6 Sprinkle the sugar onto a large plate.

7 Carefully place the banana pieces in the oil and cook for 2–3 minutes, until golden. Remove the banana pieces from the oil with a slotted spoon and roll them in the sugar. Transfer to serving bowls and serve with whipped cream or ice cream.

COOK'S TIP

Rice flour can be bought from whole-food stores or from Chinese grocery stores.

Index